CHASE OF THE WILD GOOSE

THE LADIES OF LLANGOLLEN

The Llangollen Ladies

The story of Lady Eleanor Butler
and Miss Sarah Ponsonby,
known as the Ladies of Llangollen

by
Mary Gordon

JOHN JONES

The Llangollen Ladies
by
Mary Gordon

Originally titled *Chase of the Wild Goose,* published 1936
Republished as the original text, March 1999

ISBN 1 871083 91 5

Printed by MFP Design & Print, Manchester

Cover design by Neil Angove

Published by John Jones Publishing Ltd, Unit 12, Clwydfro Business Centre,
Ruthin, North Wales, LL15 1NJ

EMMA JUNG

TO YOU, WITH AFFECTIONATE REGARDS,
THIS BOOK

CONTENTS

LIST OF ILLUSTRATIONS

AUTHOR'S FOREWORD

THE subjects of this tale, known as the Ladies of Llangollen, were real people. Lady Eleanor Butler was born 197 and Sarah Ponsonby 179 years ago. They died in 1829 and 1831, after living together, without being separated for a single day, for fifty years.

During the last 157 years all kinds of exaggerated or untrue stories have been in circulation regarding the reasons for, and the manner of their flight from Ireland. There still exists no biographical account of them which is not in one particular or another based on hearsay, phantasy, or empty conjecture, and the reconstruction of their very interesting story at this date demands the use of various artist's material. I have taken every pains to ground my tale on the things nearest to reality, preserving historical setting where it may be had, as well as genuine incidents when these are available.

The Ladies left several fragments of a delightful journal, and I have paid every regard to the attitudes, beliefs, and general psychology revealed by, or implicit in this. The existence of this journal has been known for many years. Three writers have had access to it: Mr. Charles Penruddocke, whose brochure published in 1897 is now out of print, Mr. Arthur Ponsonby, M.P., who in 1922 included some small extracts from it in his *English Diaries*, and Mrs. Eva Mary Bell, who in her book, *The Hamwood Papers*, published by Messrs. Macmillan in 1934, included all the remainder of the journal. For my purpose here, I take both parts of the journal as one.

The Hamwood Papers contain two other diaries which refer to the Ladies. I ignore that of Caroline Hamilton, granddaughter of Sir William Fownes, whose conduct obliged Sarah Ponsonby to abandon the protection of his roof. Caroline Hamilton was only born in the year in which the Ladies left Ireland, was twenty-one years younger than Sarah Ponsonby, only saw her on a few occasions late in their life, did not write of the Ladies in her journal until after their deaths, when she was not less than fifty-three years old, and although she then had in her possession the evidence of the reasons of Sarah Ponsonby's flight from Ireland, did not tell it.

The other diary, written by Mrs. Goddard, a friend of all the parties concerned, bears the stamp of naïve truth-telling and contains reliable history. Other letters from two or three people in the same circle are invaluable, showing how history, or scandal, is made. A third reliable source of material is to be found in the letters of the Ladies' friend, Miss Seward.

But the above sources of information are fragmentary, and touch only points, although important points, in the Ladies' long lives. I have made what use was possible of the little that is to be had, and for the rest have based my story on some history, some tradition, some first-hand information, contacts recorded with people of their own generation or time, things owned or made by themselves, the house and locality in which they lived so long, the colours with which they imbued their thinking, feeling and whole atmosphere, adopting scenes which were. their common experiences. I can only do justice to the main feature of the Ladies' lives, their great and abiding love for one another, by calling in the poets and letting them speak as no writer of their story could do.

As for my last chapters, each reader will interpret them according to his own opinion of ghosts.

In connection with the portraits of Lady Eleanor Butler and Sarah Ponsonby which appear in this book, I should explain that the Ladies would never have their portraits painted; but they were visited in their home from time to time by various artists of their acquaintance, and certain portraits exist which were probably done from memory, or from sketches surreptitiously made during these visits. The portrait of the two which appears here as frontispiece, will be familiar to a large number of readers. It is from an oil-painting by an unknown artist, which has been reproduced many times in prints and photographs, and is to be seen on picture postcards all over North Wales. The heads which appear facing pages 210 and 214 are taken one from this painting and one from a print of it. The portrait of a Lady in a Tall Hat, facing page 140, was at one time thought to be a portrait of Lady Eleanor Butler. It is now thought to be more probably a memory portrait of Sarah Ponsonby. This picture is now in the possession of Mrs. Whittington Herbert of Llangollen, to whom I am indebted for permission to reproduce it here.

My thanks are due to the Llangollen Town Council; to Mrs. Stanley Richards of Llangollen and to Miss Thackeray for kindly lending me characteristic letters of the Ladies; to Miss Lloyd Jones for permission to reproduce the portrait of the second Duke of Ormonde, which is in her possession; to her and Miss Mainwaring for the valuable help they have given me in obtaining information; and to various other residents in Llangollen, and those correspondents in Kilkenny, Waterford and Litchfield, who have so kindly helped me by answering enquiries on various subjects.

M. G.

Part I

THE LADIES MEET ONE ANOTHER

CHAPTER I

FIRST MEETING

THE two heroines of this story, the Lady Eleanor Butler and Miss Sarah Ponsonby, have a remarkable history. They achieved fame at a stroke. They made a noise in the world which has never since died out, and which we, their spiritual descendants, continue to echo. It is true that they never foresaw that the hum they occasioned would join itself to the rumblings of the later volcano which cast up ourselves. Suffice it that they made in their own day an exclusive and distinguished noise.

Their own day began in the middle of the eighteenth century, when nothing that they did could pass unnoticed, for they were members of two of the most powerful of those noble families that had made the destinies of Ireland, families in which each individual man and woman counted as important. The more members of a family of that kind there were, the more persons there were to make advantageous marriages and to contribute towards and augment the family riches and power, the more there were to perpetuate their noble blood and species.

In the veins of both ladies ran blood of the bluest, and behind them were long pedigrees. They had grown up into refined, capable young women of the world, and the obvious duty of each was to attain the honourable eminence that awaited her by becoming the mother of a robust brood of sons and daughters. Once engaged on this, her predestined and proper occupation, she would never be required to stop.

Sarah Ponsonby's father was Chambré Brabazon Ponsonby, grandson of the first Viscount Dungannon, and son of Major-General the Honourable Henry Ponsonby and Frances, daughter of the fifth Earl of Meath. Chambré Brabazon Ponsonby married three times, and by each wife had a daughter. Sarah was the daughter of his second wife. During the five years following her birth her mother died, her father married a third time, had his third daughter, and after begetting a posthumous son, died himself. The third wife, Sarah's stepmother, who was daughter and heiress of Sir William Barker of Kilcooley Abbey, married again. Thus, from her earliest infancy, Sarah was an orphan, and having no near relations she belonged to nobody.

Eleanor Butler was a descendant of the Earl of Ormonde. The twelfth Earl of Ormonde had been created Duke of Ormonde in Ireland in 1661, and in England in 1677. His grandson who succeeded him as second Duke, and who was Lord of the Bedchamber in the reign of James II, was, in 1746, in the reign of George I, attainted for high treason and his honours extinguished. The Irish earldom of Ormonde and Viscountcy of Thurles were vested in John Butler of Kilcash. On his death, Eleanor Butler's father, Walter Butler, became *de jure* sixteenth

THE SECOND DUKE OF ORMONDE
(From a portrait by Sir Godfrey Kneller)

Earl of Ormonde, and had the title then been restored would have assumed it as sixteenth Earl.

It was the ambition of Walter Butler and all his family to secure the restoration of the title.

Eleanor Butler, the only unmarried daughter, lived with her parents at Kilkenny Castle. Mr. and Mrs. Butler were rich, ambitious, and stupid. Their one dominant desire being to have the earldom restored, it was necessary to obtain the influence in high places which might enable them to gain their end. The people on whom they were required to make an impression were either Irish peers or English peers of strong Irish sympathies. Some of the Irish peers lived very little in Ireland, and their whole outlook was English rather than Irish. Although there was little to boast of in the moral or political standards of either country, the tendency of the Irish people to sudden political explosions was regarded by these great unattached people with natural suspicion. Walter Butler was a weak character, dominated by his wife. Mrs. Butler had a bad temper with which she ruled whatever in her world was susceptible of that kind of rule. Her casual, gloomy, untidy house swarming with undisciplined servants, was not a home for any of its occupants even when Mrs. Butler was not turning it into a blast-furnace of wrath. Like most bad-tempered people, she robbed herself of respect and of friends by her frequent breaches of common courtesy. Neither husband nor wife had any idea of how to set about gaining their end, except by the giving of extravagant entertainments, and by scheming and plotting endlessly to secure advantageous connections through

the marriages of their children. It seemed
extremely unlikely that people would take trouble
to help Mr. Butler in the matter of the earldom.
Still, his clever handsome daughter was an asset
in his striving.

In her teens Miss Butler received her education
at a French convent, for Mrs. Butler was a
Catholic and was advised that her daughter's
sojourn in France might equally advantage herself and her parents. The choir sisters of the
convent with whom she came in contact were
most of them daughters or relatives of great
French families. A few of the lay sisters were
Irish. When it became known, as the Superior
took care that it should be known, that Miss
Butler came from among the cream of Irish
aristocracy, she was visited, taken out, fêted, and
once even found herself in the presence of the
French King and Queen. Letters were written
about her to her parents which made Mrs.
Butler not only proud but jealous of her—her
charm and cleverness were subjects of continual
reference by the writers. But so much appreciation of the girl abroad made the priests who were
the Butler family advisers nervous. Had not
something of the kind been the undoing of the
Ormonde who had brought himself and his
relations to grief. Accordingly Miss Butler
was brought home again in order that she
might not gain too much foreign colour in her
ideas, nor yet be lost to her country. She came
home marvellously matured, yet with some of
the simplicity of the nuns, her late teachers,
about her. She stood somewhat aloof—there was
some invisible screen between herself and all

others. She cared very little for the society into which she was at once pressed, and had no idea of assuming the role of a popular débutante. She had nothing if not a superb and individual pride of caste which, however, her parents completely failed to realize. If they were shut away from her they had turned the key against themselves.

The desirability of her marriage presented itself to her whole family circle. Once she was safely married to a suitable man she could take a leading position among the ladies of her set. Estimating her points her relatives considered that her consuming love of Nature, of life out of doors, could be carefully directed into the cultivation of a clique given to hunting and other sports. Her interest in politics—her political sense was truly Irish in its intensity—her beauty, her vivacity, her cleverness, all these qualities were susceptible of exploitation for the advantage of her family's interests. This she knew as well as anyone else. Her life in France had informed her of the diversity of choices which were hers. She could no more have escaped growing up a woman of the world, although as yet a young one, than Sarah Ponsonby would escape it. Indeed, she had already a greater tolerance for the standards of life which she would on no account accept for herself than the young Sarah had as yet acquired.

In spite of the disadvantage she was under in being the daughter of unprepossessing, provincially-minded parents, she could have had with ease the popularity which she scorned to invoke, and could have married whenever she would. But when it was found that she declined to put

her individual interests at the service of her
relations' ambitions, and refused sound suitors,
hard epithets began to ring in her hearing.
" Eccentric," " unwomanly," or " old maidish "
—in such colours were her scruples painted. She
was asked plain questions and told home truths,
to neither of which she made answer. What was
she for ? What was any woman for ? What was
life for ? What did she propose as an alternative
to marriage ? She knew very well there was only
one and that unthinkable. She knew a woman of
quality could not live by herself. Her home—
her mother said—had had more than enough of
her. She found that she was free to lead a
frivolous life, to dress, to spend, to flirt, to run
after any man to whom she was attracted, but
was not free to read, nor to educate herself, nor
to amuse herself out of doors, without the continual nagging and depreciatory comments of
her parents. The girl, sensitive and helpless, but
always fine-mannered, suffered cruelly. But she
never failed in courtesy to all her world. Her
attitude was based on something more than the
pride of fine manners—there was an ideal behind
it. It was an additional grievance to her parents,
who called her stubborn, that no abusive words
could move her to hasty or uncivil replies even
when she had every provocation and her mother's
bitter unconscious projections rained upon her.
Not infrequently in an access of jealousy over
behaviour which she could not hope to copy
Mrs. Butler would try to correct or humiliate
her daughter before visitors or servants, only to
realize that in the end she was doing harm to her
own dearest ambitions.

Eleanor Butler was a gifted young woman. She was musical—but who could sing or play with a heart of lead ? She could write and speak the fine, stilted, accurate, and somewhat artificial English of her day. She had a brilliant grasp of contemporary history, and a taste for the best literature she could come by. But her narrow world contained no men or women with critical literary sense, nor any who wished to discuss the wider world-affairs with a woman. In solitude she worked and read, and washed her soul in the green world out of doors. For several years she bore her intolerable life with dignity and patience. But there were limits, and she had already determined that she would end it by an escape from Ireland and a plunge into the unknown world outside its borders. She realized too well the condition of French society to imagine that help lay there.

If Miss Butler in her home had hard conditions to endure, so also had Sarah Ponsonby in her own world. She could scarcely have been worse off if she had been born in the frankly polygamous surroundings of an Arab tent. Her father had married two heiresses, her older half-sister was an heiress, all her relations were rich. But she herself was left financially out of count. Whoever inherited her father's money she had none to speak of. What had happened in Sarah's case cannot be known, but in the eighteenth century in Ireland enormous fortunes were made, and often lost, or dissipated, or gambled away, and women by no means always received what was theirs or were able to keep it. No " fortune " of Sarah's would in future tempt a lover, but only her name and beguiling self. However, the legitimate offspring of great families did not get lost, and Sarah was worth while to her clan. It would pay them to bring her up and marry her to money. The rich people nearest to her brought her up, and turned out a very clever and proud girl. In her friends' view if ever a girl nurtured on the best of everything, and without ties, should be care free and willing to go like a lamb to whatever fate assigned to her, Sarah was that girl. Sarah never heard herself spoken of, or to, as though she had a mind or choices or tastes of her own, or any future whatever except as someone's wife. She was not expected to criticize the world in which she found herself, and her approval or disapproval of her social circumstances would have been to no point. From the time she was twelve years old she heard so much about marriage that by the time she was eighteen she was ignoring it, as Eleanor Butler had done.

Since the powerful families who were making Ireland's fate and history were powerful on account of their careful marriages, which preserved money in substantial blocks to be used or wasted as pleased themselves, they found it necessary to marry early, and late, and as often as possible. Individuals were always dying—often of diseases which in our own day are preventible—and there were tragic deaths in childbirth. Whenever anyone died, he or she usually left a consolable survivor. Whenever there was an inheritance, a " fortune," a good dowry, or a member of a fine family " on the make " to spare, marriage or remarriage was the obvious thing. Few men, and almost no women were allowed by their vigilant relatives to embrace a financially sterile widowhood. As a result of this greedy attitude Society was grossly selfish, and the contrasts between the lives of the rich and the poor at its gates tended to shock observers. It was tinged with a film of French fine manners, and French rationalistic thinking, both alien and artificial and corrupting.

Over and above these influences there existed a national mentality cleaved in half by two opposing factors. There were ancient Irish ideals inherited from generations of fairies, saints, and heroes who still pervaded Ireland unrealized, and there was a primitive native tendency to excesses—to orgy, that liability under moderate excitation to hit too hard and go too far—to destroy what it loved. When an individual once experienced the tension of these opposing forces he often developed a sense of oppression, of imprisonment, of longing for freedom. The self-contained thoughtful Sarah knew the longing. Eleanor Butler knew it. Before ever they met one another each was ready to commit a social crime, to brush aside and flout her appointed destiny, although neither knew that anyone else in the world felt in the same way.

When we make the acquaintance of Sarah Ponsonby she was eighteen years old. Her future had been fixed for her. In a few months' time she was to go to live with her elderly cousin, Lady Betty Fownes and her husband, Sir William Fownes, at Woodstock, Inistogue. She would be introduced into fashionable Dublin Society and a husband found for her. She was unlikely to be long on anyone's hands before she was married.

Someone had taken care of Sarah for at eighteen she was a charming self-possessed girl with a pretty face and fine manners—a girl who would have done any great family the utmost credit. Being poor, and dependent, and lonely, she was quiet, and somewhat sad-looking, but she could be lively and joyous when a bit of fun came her way. She was observant and clever and had made the very most of her education. Being under tutelage, and in what she understood to be a chrysalis stage of growth, she kept her ideas to herself. Being sweet natured she was innocent, although not ignorant of the facts of life and the world. No girl of her day could be ignorant owing to the free conversations which were heard among older women. But the great ladies about Sarah shocked her. She feared and disliked the life of which they talked, although they took pains to assure her that, since there was no other possible life, she was bound to accept and make the best of it. She resisted their conclusion, and was usually silent in their presence. She was not afraid of the larger world, and was confident that, in the end, she could steer her own course.

We meet her on the day upon which she was to make the acquaintance of the Butler family. She had been obliged by her circumstances to remain *en pension* at her school in Kilkenny during the holidays. Mrs. Walter Butler of Kilkenny Castle had been asked to notice her, and had invited her for a visit of a fortnight. The note of invitation informed her that, Mr.

By permission of Messrs. Fox, Greenhough & Company, Kilkenny

KILKENNY CASTLE FROM THE RIVER

Butler being an invalid, Mrs. Butler would have to leave her entertainment mainly to her unmarried daughter Eleanor. Sarah accepted the invitation with pleasure. Her visit promised to be exciting, for she had heard Miss Butler spoken of as an eccentric character and a " handful." She reflected that a little eccentricity on the part of the younger hostess might make an amusing diversion, and she had hitherto had no experience of a handful of anything, and was curious to see what it amounted to. As people seemed to dislike or disapprove of Miss Butler she was prepared to do the same. But as she knew she was one of her own caste she expected, whatever Miss Butler should turn out to be, to dislike her moderately only. There were loyalties in life which must be observed.

On a morning in late autumn she was conducted by her school chaperon about the town while some small purchases were made for her, and about three o'clock driven into the forecourt and left on the steps of the Castle entrance beside her covered dress basket, while her escort withdrew.

A genial Irish butler opened the door, and as the visitor entered confidently, indicating her impedimenta with a wave of her hand, he asked her name.

" Miss Ponsonby."

" I ask your pardon, madam, but the name has not been mentioned to me. Mrs. Butler is out."

" It is quite correct. I am expected. Show me in, please."

She was shown into a very large drawing-room which was, however, chilly and empty of signs of being comfortably occupied.

The house was absolutely quiet, and at the end of half an hour no one had come to welcome her. She wandered about the room looking at its decorations and contents. There were miniatures of people with very large eyes all looking exactly alike, Dresden and French ornaments, albums, portraits and mementos of the Earls of Ormonde, whose hereditary seat this great house was ; there were specimens of faded needlework but there were no books; there were chairs and couches of numerous designs but to Sarah books were more than furniture. She felt that life could never be lived in this room, it could not even contain with dignity the little portraits of the dead, it made them look too small—swallowed them.

She went to the window to look outside, but drew back as she saw a young woman crossing the lawn in the direction of the entrance door. She looked after the young woman with curiosity. She was hatless, she had a rosy face, blue eyes, and fair thick hair which curled like her own. She was strong and active. She wore unusual shoes, thick and square such as boys wore. She was smiling and talking to an enthusiastic puppy which had rushed to greet her. Then the glimpse of her was gone. Sarah hastily took her seat upon the sofa opposite the door where she would be found, decorously marooned, when rescued by some member of the family.

The young woman did not come. It could not have been Miss Butler after all!

Presently, however, there was the sound of carriage wheels, and of an arrival in the hall. A man entered who was speaking very slowly and quietly, and a woman whose voice was loud and imperious, and who was giving orders, and finding fault. As they approached the drawing-room door Sarah heard the words "coffee at once; if you don't have coffee you'll go to sleep and not be fit to dine out." Then the door opened with a burst, and the mistress of the house swept into the room. Looking round, she perceived Sarah in the act of rising from the sofa, and said in abrupt surprise, "What! Why! Its little Ponsonby."

But, as little Ponsonby stood up it became apparent that she was not little. She was well grown, and tall for her age, and her tallness was accentuated by her graceful erect bearing, and by her coat, which had a long narrow skirt and broad shoulder cape. She had a complexion of cream without much colour, expressive Irish blue eyes and an unnaturally still and reserved manner, but she put on at once the smile of pleasure proper for greeting a hostess, a smile which, however, seemed to fall off her face when the greetings were over.

She was kindly received by the noisy Mrs. Butler, and by her husband, a subdued individual who seemed to be in poor health and who had no opportunity of saying anything more.

"Just imagine," scolded Mrs. Butler into the air, "a guest being left here all alone; a nice reception I declare. What are they all thinking of?" She pealed the bell with an angry jerk. Before it ceased to ring the door flew open.

"Where is Miss Butler, Milligan?"

"Miss Butler's this moment come in the house, ma'am. Patrick has told her. She'll be here at once."

" Pour out the coffee, Milligan, and see that your master takes it."

" I will, ma'am." Milligan, looking firmly at Mr. Butler, held the door open and retired in charge of him.

" Now pray sit down, my dear," ordered Mrs. Butler, " and tell me——"

The door opened again. The young woman she had seen entered. It *was* Miss Butler, then, and how handsome! Sarah, looking at her hostess, was surprised to see her expression change as her daughter entered. There was antagonism in her frowning glance.   .

" Is this the way to receive Miss Ponsonby, Eleanor ? " she clattered. " She has waited here an hour. You knew I was out. I can't be everywhere at once——"

" I am very glad to see Miss Ponsonby," replied her daughter. " If I had known she was to be here, I shouldn't have gone out." She took Sarah's hand in a warm firm clasp, and smiled sincerely into her eyes. In her soft Irish voice she spoke again. " No question but that we shall be friends. We are friends already," said Eleanor Butler.

Where, Sarah asked herself, was the eccentric handful that was Miss Butler ? She could never have existed! This woman was charming, gracious, kind. Sarah's smile did not fall off this time, but in speechless response to the other's words she flushed delicately all over her pale face.

Mrs. Butler did not watch the greeting. She turned towards the door, saying as she went, " See that you entertain her properly," and vanished.

Eleanor Butler, still holding the young visitor's hand, scrutinized her gently. "You are fatigued," she said.

"Oh! No, I thank you."

"But yes. When did you have dinner?"

"Oh! . . . well . . . we . . . I hadn't time for it. It didn't matter at all."

"But it does matter." She went to the bell and rang it.

"Oh, Milligan, Miss Ponsonby has had nothing to eat since breakfast."

"God help the young lady," said the butler in sympathetic consternation.

"Nor have I. So we'll feast together now. Send us a tray at once, Milligan. Not downstairs —up in my sitting-room."

Milligan was well used to the kind of Irish household that ate its meals at all hours.

"What will the young lady take, ma'am?"

"Oh, cold ham, coffee with plenty of milk, scones and butter, cream, and—do you like orange preserve, Sarah? Good. Orange preserve."

"The girls is only just preparing the room for Miss Ponsonby, ma'am. They didn't know——"

"See that they put a very good fire, Milligan. Will you come with me, Sarah?"

After taking off her hat and pelisse in Miss Butler's room, the guest came through a door, as directed, to her sitting-room. Miss Butler was on her knees putting a match to the wood fire. Outside the long windows it was nearly dark, and the fire made a comfortable blaze. She rose and drew a settle near to the hearth, and smiling and pointing to a corner, said, "We can rest here."

Sitting down, Sarah said, hesitating, and un-accountably shy, " It's so good of you to call me by my name. I . . . I . . ."

Miss Butler, her voice laden with sympathy, said, " I know." She cleared a small table of an armful of books and papers and lifted it in front of the settle.

" What a beautiful large room this is," said the guest.

" Is it the room," said Miss Butler, sitting down facing her from her own corner of the settle. " Sure my heart is bigger than the room."

Suddenly Sarah's dead unknown mother seemed to be sitting beside her. She felt a great spasm of loneliness, and afraid of committing the impro-priety of showing emotion, she swallowed hard and bit her lip. And her mother's—no, it was Miss Butler's soft voice was speaking something more in her ear—" And there's a place in it for you . . . if ever . . . you want it."

Sarah let go her lip, and gave one small dry sob.

" I know," said Miss Butler again. " But I hear Patrick coming. Won't you let me see you smile ? "

Patrick himself smiled broadly as he laid the little table and handed the guest her portion. After returning with his tray to the kitchen he called the Holy Mother and all the domestic staff to note that the nice young lady that was come was making a merry meal with Miss Eleanor, who needed the weary soul within her refreshing, God knew.

After the merry meal had been cleared away, Miss Butler said: " This evening we have our time all to ourselves. No one is coming and my father and mother are going out to supper. I am wondering how I can entertain you. There are many interesting things in this house, but I do not know yet what would be likely to interest you. You must tell me your tastes."

" I am sure this splendid old house is full of treasures and that I shall enjoy it all. But I would like to know *you*, and if I may choose I would rather talk to you than do anything else. Perhaps your servants would like it if I were first to unpack my things."

" I will take you to your room and then if you will come back again we can talk for as long as we please, and have our supper sent up here by and by. It is delightful that you are here."

When Sarah returned to the sitting-room she was guided into a chair with soft cushions near the fire, and Miss Butler sank luxuriously into another at her side.

" This is so pleasant for me," she said. " We are a very quiet family here, and sometimes I hardly speak to anyone except the servants for a week. I almost forget how to talk and I am so much enjoying having you to talk to. My sister and my brother are married. They are not far away, my sister at Ballyhale, but they disapprove of me, so I am obliged to live to a certain extent in books."

" I too am lonely, and fond of reading."

" Will you tell me about your people. We heard some time ago that your stepmother was ill."

" Oh! She died in Italy six months ago. But I was not living with her. I was not with her

c

after she married Sir Robert Staples. I stayed after that at Kilcooley Abbey with her father and his wife—Sir William and Lady Barker. They were very good to me. I am fond of them."

" And then ? "

" Sometimes I went to my married half-sister, Mrs. Lowther—she is not much interested in me —and then I went to school, and I went to Kilcooley in the holidays—once to my mother's brother, Colonel Lyons—just a stranger."

" But haven't you another stepbrother and sister ? Where are they ? "

" They are at this moment at Kilcooley with their grandfather, Sir William Barker. Mary is three years younger and Chambré is five years younger than I am. He is to take the name of Barker and be Sir William's heir."

" Oh ! Then among all these relatives you have no home ? "

" No. No home. As I am no relation to the Barkers you couldn't expect them to treat me like the other two."

" Oh ! My dear Sarah ! "

" Well . . . I don't know. . . . Sometimes I am glad that no one claims me. It is lonely, but I am used to it, and even if I had parents I would rather belong to myself—now."

" Are you going to do that with the Fownes ? They'll make a slave of you——"

" Will they ? I haven't considered my future. This is as far as I have got. I don't know what next. Everyone says I must marry."

" Why, of course, your cousin Lady Betty will arrange a marriage for you."

" I should not submit to that. I shall do as I like. I shall not marry to please other people; only to please myself." Sarah's face, staring into the fire, was blank and desolate.

" It is the same with me," Eleanor Butler said, " only I have not married because I don't intend to do it——"

" Intend ? Do you mean you intend not to marry ? "

" Yes."

" Do you mean not on *any* account ? "

" Just that . . . not on any account."

" I have never heard anyone say that before."

" One doesn't say it, of course."

Sarah asked timidly, " Excuse me, but wouldn't your family be vexed ? "

" Very much vexed. But it wouldn't suit me to marry. I must own my own life. I might want to do a great many things which marriage would prevent. One has to choose."

" But . . . people may fall in love."

" Well . . . yes . . . they may. I am realizing that they could."

They were silent. Miss Butler, clasping her knee, meditated, her eyes on the fire.

" It's not a nice world for a woman," the young visitor said with a sigh. " I wonder what would make it better."

" Not falling in love—but experiencing the transforming miracle which is love."

" Oh! What a beautiful thing to say! Is it too rare to count on ? "

" I think very rare, very difficult, and probably Heaven on Earth."

Something in her companion's voice, as it

dropped, made Sarah look up at her. Miss Butler was smiling. She was also looking at Sarah with intent enquiry.

Sarah coloured slightly.

Eleanor Butler said seriously. " I think that nothing cheap, or second-rate, or *faute de mieux* will ever do for you or me."

" No. I would go without everything rather than not have . . . not have——"

" Rather than not have, and be able to give, love. I know. Oh, but what wild ideas these are, are they not ? "

" *No*," Sarah replied with emphasis. " They are *not* wild. One is a lady ! "

" You have said it. Yes. One is a lady."

When Sarah Ponsonby came to Kilkenny Castle she made an instantaneous and deep appeal to Eleanor Butler for sympathy and understanding. Sarah, equally refined in mind and soul, equally brave and full of character; Sarah, self-contained, reserved and with her adult life unlived; Sarah, wholesome and hopeful, was dreaming of a world which she could find very good. During their two weeks spent together Sarah became a momentous and entirely confounding fact in Eleanor's life. How was she herself to flee away in the ship of destiny if Sarah were going to control the anchor ?

The two friends treated one another with the reserve that is more common among boys. Eleanor listened attentively to all that Sarah told her of her life and conditions, showed that she understood her, but asked her no questions. Sarah witnessed enough of the injustice and persecution suffered by Eleanor to feel for her acutely, but respected her absolute silence over her grievous conditions. No two young women could have been less sentimentally inclined. Life was pressing on each too heavily to be eased by sentiment. They did not express their real understanding of one another through personalities; general ideas of life and the world took up their time. Both had a deep love of Nature and an interest in plants and animals, both loved books, both had the instincts and perceptions of artists, and a keen appreciation of beautiful and significant things. There was immense meaning and value for both in these preoccupations which could be shared with one another and so made doubly delightful.

Ideals gripped them. Both were proud of their descent and drawn together by the cords of social status. In the time during which they talked together they defined for one another the attitude that a high-born lady should take, not only to her kind (they quickly passed that point, possibly because it contained some thorns and resisted handling) but to the world of all human contacts.

Their friends might indeed have been astonished if on any evening in the room upstairs they could have seen these two, each in her corner of the settle before the fire, striving to express that which so many people are content to leave undefined all their lives. It would certainly have conveyed nothing to Mr. Butler drinking his wine and spirits, nor to Mrs. Butler slumbering in her armchair below-stairs.

They talked of the attitude of the hypothetical perfect lady, seeking for a formula.

"Could it be expressed?" asked Eleanor Butler tentatively, "as Live and Let Live?"

Sarah said, "Isn't it something more?"

After an interval Eleanor said, "Do we mean a sort of extension of *noblesse oblige*?"

"Perhaps a spiritual extension," said Sarah, "but no, *noblesse oblige* goes all the way to the stars."

"And beyond, perhaps," said Eleanor.

"And to the end only concerns oneself—it's rather splendid!"

In their tranquil talks their ideas seemed to coincide and fit together, and it was curious how they dropped the artificial style of their day and education. In the spiritual company of many other unknown women, they were slipping forward into another social epoch of which they were entirely unconscious pioneers.

"Nice girl, Miss Ponsonby," said Eleanor's father to his daughter towards the end of Sarah's visit. "Well brought up—good style. Your mother and I like her. And she does you good Eleanor, brisks you up—you look less moped. That family could do much for us if they chose. Ask her to come again when she can. Perhaps you could bring her over for a Sunday sometimes, and get her back to her school early on Monday."

The day came when Sarah had to be returned to her school. In a few months' time she was to go to her new home with Lady Betty Fownes at Woodstock, Inistogue. She made her polite speeches and adieux and Mrs. Butler, who had seen very little of her, and who liked her, and thought she might be a possible strand of influence by and by, cordially invited her to come again.

Eleanor Butler went with her to the school in the family coach, returning alone.

As they neared their destination Sarah turned to her. She put out both her hands and said, " I hate to go."

Eleanor took the hands in hers. " Some day," she said, " you shall not have to go any more."

" Oh! tell me what you mean."

" I don't know, Sarah. But just that! "

" From now onwards I . . . won't you keep me . . . in your heart ? "

" Don't you know you are in it ? I think you have been in it since before we were born."

CHAPTER II

ELEANOR GOES TO LONDON

A FEW months after Sarah's visit, Mrs. Butler's
harassed director, the Reverend Father Molloy,
wrote to the Catholic Archbishop of Cashel,
who was Walter Butler's uncle, and told him in
confidence that if things went on as they were
going at Kilkenny Castle he was really afraid
that Mrs. Butler would become crazy. Her
tempers were something terrible. Something
would have to be done about Miss Butler. A
young lady might be as long-suffering as this
one, but he did not see how she was to bear it.
Would His Grace not come over to the Castle
and discuss it? The gentlemen who had failed
to secure Miss Butler's hand were now married
to other ladies, and no one else, as far as was
known to her family, seemed to be coming
forward. If the family wanted her to be married
he thought she should be sent to fresh matrimonial pastures. But her parents would not let
her move away from Kilkenny. They seemed to
be afraid of her doing them harm if they did not
watch her all the time.

The Archbishop, known to his relatives as
Uncle Christopher, answered the summons after
a few days by coming to the Castle. He arrived

in a benign state of mind, looking very handsome and curiously like his great-niece.

If Eleanor had been baptized in the Catholic Church and as a child caused to frequent it, nothing had been seen or heard of her religion since she had returned from France, grown up. This indifference was not regarded by the great families of that time as important in women as yet unmarried. Father Molloy had been given clearly to understand that Holy Church would receive a handsome present if the right suitor, whether Catholic or Protestant, should secure Miss Butler's hand. The Archbishop noted her respectful attitude and address towards himself, which was everything that was correct. He had not seen her for a year or two, and was surprised and even a trifle subdued by the dignity with which she did her share in entertaining him. She was clearly a woman of the world, but in trying to estimate her character he was puzzled by her simplicity and obvious sincerity. He believed that, as a rule, rich clever women lacked these graces. The priest had told him of her good temper and patience, and as he had a profound dislike of Mrs. Butler, he was the more inclined to do something to save her daughter from her. When they rose from five o'clock dinner, and Eleanor had excused herself and retired, he introduced the subject of her continued celibacy, and listened to Mrs. Butler's outpourings on the subject until her husband at last checked them.

Then addressing Mr. Butler, he said, " Walter, I am going to suggest a new line for you to take with your daughter. Why not send Eleanor for a year to London ? "

" London ? London ? "

" Yes. If she will not do anything for her family in Ireland, let her, at least, work for it where the chances may be more favourable. You know very well that marriages are easily made between people of different nationalities. If you were to send her back to France she might readily marry a Frenchman—apparently she has a large interest in that nation—and as we are situated that would never do. But there are plenty of Irish families in high places in London. Some of them who never come to Ireland, are nearly, or altogether, English. The English would go mad over such a beautiful girl. If you sent her to London, I could arrange with the clergy and others, that she meets the men of influence who can advance your interests. You might get a fairly solid vote in the Lords. Well now—as to dowry. Could you suggest a figure for quotation ? "

" I could go to ten thousand—perhaps twelve."

" Ten should do it. The Church will deserve something if we bring it off. Now—you consider the plan, Walter."

The Archbishop paused to allow his words to sink into Mr. Butler's cloudy mind.

" Perhaps," ventured Father Molloy, " Miss Butler *may* have been held in a little tightly here at home, the young lady of spirit that she is."

" Precisely," said the Archbishop. " You send her where she can have a fling, Walter. The men we want will be about her at once. They'll come to you and you'll make a bargain, believe me. And all for her good."

" How could it be done ? "

" Well, some lady will escort her to London, and we can find another to chaperon her. And then—give her rope and she will hang herself—eh ? Ha! ha! what I mean is, send her as a woman of quality, not a second-hand débutante. Dress her. Finance the fling well."

" She's beautiful when she's dressed, and lively," said Eleanor's father feebly.

" She is," agreed Mrs. Butler impartially. " She can sparkle like a diamond, and keep a whole room entertained with that tongue of hers. Sure it's a great idea, Your Grace."

" Well then, carry it out. Of course she should not know we have discussed the matter together. You should allow the half of a month to pass before it is mentioned to her. Meantime, Walter, I will have a friendly talk with her, and try to discover where her personal difficulties and dispositions lie."

" The creature! " said Father Molloy, who would not for the world have made such inquisition himself. A few ripostes with Miss Butler's sharp rapier had long ago defined his place for him as beyond her horizon.

Next morning Uncle Christopher had a pleasant talk with his great-niece, the subject being politics. He was surprised to find how well informed she was on public affairs, and how loyal, as he was himself, to the English government. He commended her views warmly, but was careful not to speak too favourably of English people. Gradually he led the conversation towards marriage. Before they arrived at that point in the discussion, Eleanor, who saw through his intentions, changed her seat to one more directly opposite him. The Archbishop no more liked being scrutinized directly in a good light than do most of us, and had to remind himself how insignificant the scrutiny of a young ignorant woman, when directed upon a pillar of the Church, really was. He was prepared to be infinitely patient with such young women—he knew his power over them in the end.

" My child," he said, " is it not more than time that you were married ? "

Miss Butler smiled upon him pleasantly, as though the idea were entirely acceptable to her, but made no reply.

" My dear," said the prelate gently, " tell me. Is there no good man who would please you ? "

" I do not know any man well enough to be able to call him ' good '."

" Your mother tells me you have had three advantageous offers from suitable men."

" Ah! ' advantageous '—and ' suitable.' *I* am the person to be advantaged and suited. They were all out of the question."

" Perhaps you may not have given them the opportunity of showing you what was good in themselves. A woman can bring out the best that is in a man."

He received no reply, and went on. " Let me tell you, my dear Eleanor, as one who knows the world of men and women, that a woman may be too severe. If you will not allow a man to make a little love to you, which your mother tells me is the case, you cannot know—you cannot learn . . ."

The Archbishop's fatherly speech tailed away

to nothing, for his hearer was not smiling now.
Her brows were contracted, her head was drawn
back, and she was looking at him with narrow
eyes as though he were an on-coming wasp.
He changed his ground. " Er . . . what is
your objection to marriage ? "

" None. Why should I object ? But the time
and choice are mine, are they not ? "

" It looks as though you never would choose."

" It does indeed! Entirely, most Reverend
Father! My friends should accept the indica-
tion."

" It is a woman's Christian duty to marry.
What is to become of you else ? "

" I do not agree that it is my duty. I belong
first of all to myself."

" You know, daughter, that you are not happy
here. You would be far happier, and more free,
if you married as God intended you to do, and
took an assured position in the world. What
profit is there in staying on in your father's
house where you are miserable ? Or in living
and dying an old maid ? A woman of your name
and standing too, from whom the world, as well
as your family, looks for more than that! You
ought to consider what you might do for your
family—more than any other member of it."

" I shall no doubt give the world something to
look at. I find the condition of ' old maid,' as
you call it, to my taste. Although I do not
consider the expression a very refined one for use
by an archbishop to a lady. I need not stay here."

" Then what do you intend to do, Eleanor ?
Do you desire to enter religion—an Irish or
French convent ? "

" No. Absolutely not."

" Then, my dear, do tell me what is in your mind. I want to help you. I do indeed."

" What I have in my mind has come of long consideration. In my own time it will end in action. Meantime, may I beg you to excuse me from replying to any more questions; I have reached my limit. I am grateful to you, but there is no way in which you can help me."

" If it is the difficulty of your parents, which I fully appreciate——"

" Pardon me, but I never discuss my parents with other people. I live under their roof, and eat their bread. You may take it from me that I have my own faults——"

The Archbishop admired her, and felt for her more than she knew. Once, years ago, his own family had resented his celibate calling. He now felt certain that his suggestion to transfer her to London was the best thing that could be done for her, and for everyone concerned. He said kindly : " Very well, I will not say anything more. You shall be left alone." He hesitated. " Will you accept my blessing ? "

Eleanor Butler dropped on her knee to receive it. As she stood upright again, he said, " I will pray for you. Good-bye, my dear child." He held out his hand. There was cold blue fire in Eleanor's eyes as she held her hands dropped at her sides. She spoke with deliberation and without temper.

" No, Archbishop," she said quietly. " I can do with your prayers, but I do not shake hands with any man who shows me that he would sell me in the usual market for thirty pieces of silver, or for a handful of votes from the Lords." She added, "You have spoken of 'making love,' but not of Love, for which I thank you." She turned and left the room.

The Archbishop was sincere, but something in his soul stabbed him unaccountably. He told himself that it must be sorrow for the girl's naïve impertinence and conceit, but he felt as though he had trodden on a bird. He was agitated, his heart thumped a little, and his ordinarily dry hands were sweating.

When he had recovered his equanimity he sought Father Molloy and detailed to him his want of success with the family handful. And he said reflectively, "She's torn in two by *something*."

"If a girl is under such special protection of the Holy Virgin as that one," replied Father Molloy, "and refuses to enter Religion where she'd make a real holy nun, I ask you whether she wouldn't be torn in two, God help her."

The Archbishop saw his great-niece again before he left the Castle. She came to see to his comfort, and to ask him whether he would take a meal before he started on his journey, or would prefer to take a packet of luncheon with him.

Instead of replying to her question, the Archbishop stood looking at her, inviting her by his friendly smile to respond to it.

"I like your spirit, Eleanor. I will remember that you are a great lady."

"Great ladies expect to converse with gentlemen. As a lady, I apologize. I ought not to have said and done what I did. Will you . . ." She offered her hand.

As he took it the Archbishop said, "And I would like to be the kind of gentleman that the great lady approves. I will try to deserve her. Will she . . ."

She would. Uncle Christopher kissed her forehead and crossed himself and blessed her; in his heart he admired her generous amends, and went away asking his Lord to make him a less worldly man.

When Uncle Christopher had gone back to his diocese, Mr. and Mrs. Butler talked over his proposal.

"There's great sense in it," said Mrs. Butler, prepared to gamble afresh with her daughter as the stake.

"It could be a dead loss," said Mr. Butler pessimistically.

"Loss, is it ? Look at the way the rents are coming in. You could give her a thousand and never know you'd done it." She added, " She wouldn't take jewels from me, but I can give her sister some fine ornaments for her. God knows it will be a rest to me to be without her for a time." Mrs. Butler emitted the sigh of a martyr.

"I suppose it is a father's part," said Walter Butler, drearily. "Very well. I'll speak to her next week, and you can write to her sister. She might go with her perhaps to London."

The suggestion that she should go to London was entirely acceptable to Eleanor Butler. It might be very useful to her plans for the future. In what seemed to her fairness, she reminded her mother that as far as her marriage was concerned nothing was likely to come of it, since she proposed to remain single. Mrs. Butler, whose own dreams were now foremost in her mind, laughed indulgently and told her not to be foolish, nor to think she knew better than ' nature.' " And you'll not remain single in your father's house, Eleanor. It will be a convent for you, my girl, unless you learn sense. Your father won't have you disgracing us here."

The plan could not, however, be given effect at once, and nearly a year passed before it was arranged that Eleanor should go to an old family friend, Lady Hartskill, and the preparations for her departure began.

" No use fitting you out here," said Mrs. Butler. " The fashions don't come to Kilkenny. You have very good taste, and Lady Hartskill will advise you. Your father wishes you to make a good appearance for all our sakes. Here is money, and he has also sent a draft for £500 to a London bank for you. No doubt you will meet some of your fine French friends of whom you think so much. I'm told the ladies are most elegant. Don't let them outshine you. And don't forget to introduce the question of the title if you meet anyone who is interested. You might have great opportunities of doing something. I should like to see you Lady Eleanor yourself one day."

" No one can desire that more than I do," replied her daughter. " But I think it very unlikely that anything could be done. This is too much money; I should never spend it."

" It's yours. You needn't account for it."

" I have had an invitation from Lady Betty Fownes to spend a day and night at Woodstock on my way to join the travelling party."

D

" Accept it then. It is as well to be civil to all
that family."

For a year Sarah had been living with Sir
William and Lady Betty Fownes. She had seen
Eleanor twice and had corresponded with her
during the whole period, and a great intimacy
and deep affection had sprung up between them.
They spoke now of one another's affairs, and
occasionally of that vague improbable " some-
day " which had a prominent place in both their
minds. If Lady Betty Fownes never guessed the
depth of their young friendship, neither did the
jealous, contrary Mrs. Butler. Their correspondence was conducted secretly, not because they
themselves had arranged it, but because they
had round them a fairy ring of unseen protectors.
The Castle servants, a sensitive long-suffering
company, were united in their attachment to
their young Mistress Eleanor, and the two head
menservants, Milligan and Patrick, soft-hearted
tactful Irishmen, had seen the development of
her friendship with Miss Ponsonby. The letters
received and dispatched by Miss Butler were
delivered to her and collected when no one was
about. At Woodstock the letters sent by Miss
Ponsonby, or received by her, were carefully
guided to their destination by Lady Betty's maid,
Mary Carryl. This was not in response to a
taste for conspiracy, but in order that the new
young lady might be safeguarded from those
prying enquiries which the servants in both
houses regarded as an intolerable tyranny to
which young ladies were unjustly subjected.

The ladies of that day, although often none too
literate, were correspondents at a length and to

an extent unknown nowadays. The casual irregular posts carried streams of gossiping letters
to London or to Ireland. The matter which the
journals or newspapers could not supply of
political, or court, or fashionable news, was
supplied in abundance by ready private pens.
The habit induced in the more selective and
intelligent minds a wider, more cosmopolitan,
outlook than stay-at-home Irish husbands and
fathers usually possessed, and again on the part
of the writers was a sliding into a more advanced
epoch unrealized by themselves. And so, although
it was known that the two friends had acquired
the habit of corresponding at what appeared to
be rare intervals, no one connected it with their
love for one another. Love was a thing which a
man spent on a woman and a woman spent on
her children, and was a luxury, not a necessity.
In any case, it was only spread about on sheets
of letter-paper by very romantic and foolish
scribes. Protests of esteem were, however, in all
letters brought to a fine art, and were mainly
decorative features of correspondence, like capital
letters.

Eleanor, the intuitive, was not deceived by
Sarah Ponsonby's description of her happy idle
life. She did not believe it could last, but meantime Lady Betty was kind and motherly and Sarah
loved her. She was also fond of Lady Betty's
married daughter, Sarah Tighe, and (which was
very odd of Sarah) of Lady Betty's old friend
Mrs. Goddard, a phenomenal Irish widow who
had not married again. While she was in London,
Eleanor reflected that at any rate Sarah would
be safely housed and cared for. She was very

sorry to hear that Sarah was having to scrutinize at close quarters the unkindness and bad temper of her temporary guardian, Sir William Fownes, towards his placid little wife. She was unwilling that Sarah should be dismayed with the idea of marriage, as she, in her own home, had been dismayed by what she had seen of it.

In their talk on their last morning together, Eleanor told Sarah that she did not believe she would have a home with her parents on her return from London. There had been some threats of a convent, and of course she should not consent to that. Rather, she would cast herself into the world as an independent individual— earn an honest living somehow.

" That would be terrible, Eleanor. It's not done."

" It would have to be done."

" But . . . but . . . how should we live, be able to get enough to live on ? "

" We ? *We ?* "

" Yes," said Sarah with sudden passion, " *we.* Am I to part with you ? I . . . I . . . couldn't."

Eleanor looked at her dumb and stricken.

" I want nothing else but you. I hate my life. It's all idleness and sham, eating and drinking and playing cards, and the most horrid gossip. Am I to grow old like the women round about me ? What of the things we have talked of and dreamt of ? Where is *noblesse oblige,* where is freedom, where is life ? "

Sarah was sobbing uncontrollably.

" All on the knees of the gods, Sarah," said the other mournfully. She drew the girl's head on her shoulder and pressed away her tears.

" Hush, my dear. Hush, my own, someone might hear us. There . . . there . . . dry your eyes and let us talk while we may. There! Don't cry again, it breaks my heart in pieces."

Sarah stopped crying with an effort, and asked again :

" Then, how could we live ? "

" Well, families like our own can be very cruel, but they wouldn't allow ladies belonging to them to go begging. That would be a scandal it would not pay them to make. You and I are entitled to the support of our own people. Society, who will not let us do anything else, knows it. We should probably be given enough to keep us alive."

" You perhaps."

" And you. Where is the share of your father's estate which you, his second daughter, should have ? "

" I wouldn't ask for it."

" Well, while I am away, think of the cost of liberty, Sarah. Loss of the friends of our order, perhaps loss of one another, perhaps we should have to endure illness in poverty—and poverty for life. I should destroy my parents' hopes, and they would never forgive me. We should go on what the world calls a wild-goose chase. Could I take you to such a life ? "

" I want to hear you say I may chase the wild goose with you. God would help us."

" Well, we must wait a little longer until you are of age. Then—if you want me—I will come for you. I only hesitate to expose you to all the difficulties. But I promise you that after this time we will never part again. You are all the world to me, Sally."

" What will you do in London, Eleanor ? "

" Be assured I shall be building for our future. Also refusing the English beaux specially introduced to me." She laughed. " My mother tells me I am to have a big dowry on my marriage. No doubt she will secure that Lady Hartskill makes it known. I shall be placed at auction, Sally! "

" How horrid it is! "

" Pooh! I shall not know anything about it." Sarah said. " Although I refused those two men—they were not even young, you know— Lady Betty promises me that I shall in the end meet my fate, but *I* can promise *her*———"

" Don't promise anything. You know, Sally, the men have a right to love you and every inducement to do it. Listen to what any man wishes to say to you. Remember his feelings— *noblesse oblige*, eh ?—and treat him with respect and kindness. As Lady Betty says, you may meet with someone whom you desire to accept. There are lovable men in the world and marriage is natural and right. We think—you and I— that we want something strange and exceptional, but something different *may* be ordained for us. Try to earn the sincere respect of the men you meet."

" I like you so much better than any of them."

" And I like you. But I could not give you every kind of happiness, you know."

" I rather like the Englishmen I have met," reflected Sarah.

" I like them too. They are not everlastingly thinking of money and marriages of convenience. They seem always to marry to please themselves, and not their relations."

The door opened and a servant announced that the carriage awaited Miss Butler.

" Oh, Eleanor! You must go ? "

" Yes. And now, my dear, stand up, like the fine soldier your father was—and your grandfather was—and smile—and kiss me—and wish me good fortune. I count on you to grow very good and wise. That's my brave girl! May all the Saints stand round you, dear one. I must go to Lady Betty. Don't come—she mustn't see tears. That's my darling."

She turned towards the door.

" Oh, good-bye, Eleanor. Good-bye."

Eleanor turned again with her hand on the door, smiling.

" Not good-bye, Sally. For you and me there is no such word in any world."

CHAPTER III

DEFEAT OF THE MATCH-MAKERS

WHILE Eleanor was gone to a life which Sarah would have loved to share with her, the joyous life of fashionable London, Sarah's existence was rooted in Kilkenny with an occasional change to Dublin. Lady Betty's one daughter, Mrs. Tighe, was married and occupied with her children, and Sarah took the place of daughter in the Woodstock household. She went with Lady Betty on long rounds of calls upon her friends, she played at cards, she attended balls and other entertainments, and did her best to be an amiable and helpful companion. If after a time she found herself becoming tired of the life she led, she did not let her kind little hostess know it. Lady Betty and her husband were very good to her. They gave her pocket-money and pretty dresses, and allowed her to follow her own pursuits in her spare time. They were diligent in introducing her to their world. Sarah's grace and charm quickly attracted the attention of that world, as well as the fact that, although a dowerless orphan, she was an item in a powerful family.

Sir William Fownes was a member of the Irish Parliament, and every second year spent some months at his Dublin residence during the Parliamentary session. They would be moving

to Dublin before long and then there would be
less time for the studies which she tried to keep
up.

Lady Betty—good-natured and conventional—
knew her duty towards bright affectionate Sally
Ponsonby. She had it in her power to call the
attention of eligible men to Sarah, but here
her skill ended, for she was unable to impress
her young relative with the seriousness of her
situation, and with the importance of offers for
her hand. Her task was still to induce Sarah to
accept one of the available proposals of marriage.

Two worthy men had tried their best to make
Sarah their own, but both had gone away dis-
appointed. With the perfect calm of a woman
who knew her own mind she had rejected both
absolutely. After the second suitor had retired
discomfited, Lady Betty began a serious conversation with Sarah on the subject. Looking concerned and bewildered, and singularly like a
small hen in charge of a fine young hawk, she
said, " My dear Sally, I don't understand your
objection to Mr. Rodes. Such a charming man
and thorough gentleman, who would have made
you so happy ! What *is* your objection ? "

" One doesn't trouble to ' object ' to a man who
is simply not in one's view at all. Why do you
offer a girl of twenty a man old enough to be her
father ? "

" Oh, my dear Sally, what a way to speak !
Mr. Rodes is only middle-aged, and they make
such good, kind, generous, husbands. It is done
every day." Being without much tact, Lady
Betty proceeded to give instances.

" Of course," reflected Sarah, " if a husband

is not a success there are not so many years to
face——"

" Sarcasm does not become you, Sally."

" I humbly beg your pardon. I really mean it
when I say that I neither wish to be married nor
to hear from any gentleman on the subject."

" Oh, but my dear, you really must be serious!
Remember you have no fortune. Mr. Rodes
does not mind about that. He fell in love with
you for yourself, out of genuine esteem for my
Sally's sweet qualities. What could you desire
more ? You know you must consider your future,
and what people will think."

Sarah was silent. She realized that she could
not stay for ever dependent on dear, soft, little
Lady Betty and her husband. She had no
practical alternative to offer to which they were
likely to listen.

Presently she said, " I am afraid I am hard to
please. If any other gentleman comes to you
or to Sir William about me I would rather that
you should stop him at once from any further
advance."

" That would not do, Sally. Gentlemen would
think it very odd if, while being in Society, and
amusing yourself with them, you were not . . .
er . . . were not——"

" In the market ? "

" What ails you, my dear ? What an observa-
tion to make! No one offers to buy or sell you,
my foolish Sally. But if you intend to refuse
another offer, I think you must do it yourself.
It would embarrass and inconvenience me too
much both to present you to Society and announce
your reservation. Such things are not done."

" Well then—I suppose I am able to do it."
Sarah's little laugh was detachment itself.

" You take it too lightly, Sarah. A girl must
show modesty, my dear."

" I am sincerely sorry if any man should feel
encouraged to hope for what I have no intention
of conceding. It seems to me unfair to let him
get so far."

When Sir William heard of it he stamped his
foot at his wife.

" The young fool," he said. " You must give
the next applicant license to make free love to
her. And keep away from them yourself. She
would soon learn all she needs. A man is ham-
pered by negotiating with a chaperon over a
backward girl."

" If I connived at anything unbecoming,
William, her friends might be very angry. It is
a responsibility which——"

" Unbecoming! Pshaw! " said Sir William.

But Sarah was not backward. She was equal
to her world in everything except opportunity
to live the life of her choice. Being very fond of
Lady Betty and sheltered under her motherly
wing, she disliked having to be an ugly duckling
and having to hurt and confuse her. But Lady
Betty was also involved in her recoil from the
subject of marriage. She had contributed to its
black appearance several times. When the
unattached Mrs. Goddard came to stay at
Woodstock, Sarah, seated in the window and
seemingly absorbed in her drawing or French
studies, heard with amazement the conversation
they carried on, heard how Lady Betty rallied
her old friend and urged her to matrimonial

designs on an old man of sixty-seven. She, who had admonished Sarah to remember modesty, herself advised Mrs. Goddard to make the proposal to marry to the old man. While these two old friends laughed and joked over Mrs. Goddard's anomalous situation, that of a well-to-do widow, Sarah, listening in silence, shivered, and recalled something that Eleanor Butler had once said about the transforming miracle that was Love. If these two elderly women had ever known that, could they have forgotten it, or how could they smirch it with this buffoonery.

As a matter of fact, Mrs. Goddard was liked by, and was in demand among other women, and also among men. What she asked of the world were good meals and creature comforts generally. In a world full of people with ulterior motives she was a useful go-between or interpreter, she did not quarrel, she extracted amusement from others, and carried them the news. She was requisitioned by her friends to unravel domestic complications, and to perform various tasks to which they were unequal, just as they called on strangers to lay out their dead for burial. She had an entirely unemotional and totally unmoral outlook upon life. As often as not she was mistaken and ineffective, having neither judgment nor intuition, but only a weasel-like sharpness of perception, and a fearless tongue. Her mistakes were unperceived and her personal escapes from criticism or from serious blame were remarkable : she seemed to be protected by the powers that look after the conscienceless. She appreciated her unattached life of freedom and maintained it, and so imparted courage to those who, like Sarah and Lady Betty, were in bondage. This was probably the secret of their liking for, and trust in her. Mrs. Goddard however could only in reality be explained as a classical and ancient figure—the wise woman, or witch, of primitive society, to whom people irresistibly turned for help, ignoring her repulsive self.

Following the two rejected suitors, a fine young man of noble but impecunious family presented himself at Woodstock, announcing himself to Sir William and Lady Betty as desperately in love with what he had heard of Miss Ponsonby. On learning that she could contribute nothing towards his support his passion abated immediately, and it was never necessary to inform Sarah of his existence.

At this point Lady Betty suggested to Sir William that they might without inconvenience endow Sarah with, say, five thousand pounds, in order to encourage her to contemplate marriage more favourably, but he sourly refused the suggestion. He seemed to take less and less interest in Sarah's matrimonial prospects.

A few months previously, when they were in Dublin, Lady Betty had noted that a certain Captain Moriarty was continually looming in Sarah's wake. He was somewhat plebeian in appearance, speech, and manner, red-haired, ripe for orgy, but handsome, with a distracting Irish smile, and dark eyelashes flecked with gold that curled unbelievably. He was a beautiful dancer and on many occasions succeeded in leading the popular Miss Ponsonby, demure and impersonal but showing her enjoyment, in

minuet and quadrille, and once, at a masked
ball, had danced a reel with her with marked
distinction.

He came of obscure family, but was very rich.
In the eyes of his young partners his dancing
absolved him from certain defects of breeding,
and it seemed to the mortified Lady Betty that,
if made over by the fastidious and capable Sarah,
he might be permitted to pass with his money
into her superior social sphere. After hearing
from Mrs. Goddard and others praises of her
performances with the equally good dancer Miss
Ponsonby, he took courage to make a venture
which he had longed to make for some time. He
presented himself at Woodstock in quest of Miss
Ponsonby's hand.

"And really, William," said Lady Betty, "as
there seems to be no chance of doing better, I
think we might do worse. Sarah would be better
off than any of her relations—as well off as we
are ourselves, and better."

Sir William, seeing that it had to come, grunted
only.

"And I shall do as you suggest, William. I
shall say nothing at all to Sally, until he is on
the spot, and shall afford him unlimited opportunity."

At the succeeding interview Lady Betty smiled
so sweetly upon Captain Moriarty, that he
behaved humbly and sincerely, and impressed
her, on the whole favourably. Her only anxieties
were lest Sarah should reject this eligible young
man.

The young man said, "It is true I am a younger
son, my lady, but you have to put against that

the large fortune I inherited from my uncle, which leaves me better off than my elder brother."

" You were your uncle's favourite, then ? "

" I wouldn't say that," said the applicant, frankly. " It's God's truth he didn't like any of us. But a family is a family——"

" As far as Miss Ponsonby's relatives are concerned, Captain Moriarty, your aspirations are approved. If Miss Ponsonby has little fortune of her own, you realize that the standing of her family is of the best. She has an exceptionally charming personality which has already brought us several offers for her hand. As she is still unattached, I shall do all I can to show her how advantageous a match, and how happy a life you offer her."

" Refused several offers ? Is she then the kind of young lady who could play fast and loose with a man ? "

" Oh, my dear Captain Moriarty, by no means. So far she has been indifferent to all aspirants. She is young and unformed in her ideas and shows no inclination to the married state. Indeed I have not, up to the present, prevailed upon her to think seriously of it at all. We may have been too formal, but, to satisfy you, I shall leave you full and free opportunity of approaching her, and pressing your suit. Come here as often as you wish. I should counsel you to approach her with chivalry, very gently and tentatively, as becomes a young man seeking to affect the delicate sensibilities of a refined, inexperienced girl. You apprehend my meaning I am sure."

" I do, my lady. You counsel me to proceed

slowly and not—as it were—to carry the position by storm."

" Quite so. Treat her very seriously, and take plenty of time."

" Your ladyship knows I have met Miss Ponsonby in society already nearly a dozen times, and think the present time as suitable as any time is likely to be. But—if I have to cajole the young lady to the extent you estimate it would be the first time that a girl—that a young lady—put such a lagging task on me."

Lady Betty replied with dignity, " I speak because I wish you well. Whatever your experience may have been, you will pardon me if I suggest that you are too young a man to have had great experience with ladies of good family and education. I venture to warn you that Miss Ponsonby is not the kind of young lady you meet with every day. She is exceptionally high spirited and well educated, and estimates her own value highly. Let me advise you to meet her with respect on her own ground. Extraordinary as it may seem, I do not think your large fortune will serve your turn at all, and you may safely neglect to speak of it."

Something deep and new-born in Lady Betty's soul was making her care that Sally should *not* be bought or sold. She got up and rang the bell. " Ask Miss Ponsonby to come to me in the library please."

They waited, and Captain Moriarty said, " On my honour you make me nervous, my lady."

" That is good. Then you will be careful."

As Sarah entered Lady Betty said, " My dear, Captain Moriarty has just called. I think you may remember having met him last winter. He wishes to speak to you." She went out closing the door.

Sarah affected surprise. " To *me*, Captain Moriarty? " She shook hands ceremoniously and sat down on a chair.

Captain Moriarty felt his brain reeling and his heart galloping. She really was a Queen! He stood before her and said stammering, " And a difficult thing it is, Miss Sarah. I don't know how I am going to say it."

" You have not, I fear, heard my name correctly. It is Ponsonby. Seat yourself, I beg. How can I serve you ? "

Embarrassed, the suitor began explosively, " A thousand pardons, Miss S-S—Ponsonby, er . . . the fact is . . ." (precipitately) " You have me knocked to your adorable feet."

" Do you *know* what you want, Captain Moriarty ? "

The suitor seized the opening with simplicity. " It's your own lovely self, to be sure."

"May I ask what you would do with me ? "

Grateful for so much help he became cheerful. " Why, make you the best husband in the world. Take all care of you. Open your eyes in Paradise, worship the stones you step on . . ."

He rose and came towards her.

" Oh! I thank you. Remain seated if you please. I am sensible of the very great honour you do me, and am sorry indeed to disappoint you, but there is nothing for you here." As he looked stunned, she added, " I am not able to accept what you offer me."

" What is it would tempt you to consider it, Miss S-Ponsonby ? "

E

" I am afraid nothing. I have other ideas."

" If it's plenty of freedom you would be wanting. . . ."

" I have now all the freedom I want."

" Sure now, Miss Ponsonby, I'm just dying of love for you."

The young man's earnestness gave him dignity which she admired.

" Say you'll agree to giving me just a shade of hope. Don't turn me right off . . . when you know me . . . you needn't take me . . . if you find you don't . . . like me." His voice, vibrating with feeling, called for pity and he had it.

" *No.* I cannot consent to say I will contemplate a thing which I have not any intention at all of doing. It would be dishonourable of me to keep you in suspense. I am very sorry, but it cannot be. You must go away and forget your idea."

" I'm more likely to jump in the river or blow out my brains with misery."

" What! A man as full of life as you are ? You know very well you won't do anything of the sort! That is for foolish people! " Miss Ponsonby laughed—an indulgent little laugh.

Gone was all Lady Betty's exhortations.

The lover lost his head. He edged his chair nearer hers.

" You pretty little witch, you! You bright-eyes! May I call here sometimes ? "

" No, thank you . . . I would rather you did not."

" Then take the edge off despair for me. Say good-bye to me with one little kiss. Do! It will be the world to me. Do, now! "

"And leave off being ridiculous, please."
Miss Ponsonby rose and pushed back her chair.

The lover said, with a groan, "Oh! My God! I'm the unfortunate man."

"Before you propose to a lady, Captain Moriarty, you should make sure that neither you nor her friends are making bids for money or position."

"Believe me your friends have not, Miss Ponsonby. And whatever a man's riches may be, the like of you is above all money value. He *couldn't* buy you."

He looked at her completely sobered, and seeing compassion in her face he had a sudden intuition.

"May I ask you," he said earnestly, "if there's another gentleman unknown to your friends——"

"In strictest confidence, Captain Moriarty, there *is* someone else before you to whom I am pledged."

"Oh! Lady! Have I insulted you?" There were tears in his eyes.

"Oh, no, no! But that caps all, and closes the subject, doesn't it. I wish you well." Seeing his emotion, she said kindly, "You will like to let yourself out, will you not? Good-bye." She shook hands with him. "There is your hat on that table. Good-bye."

When he had gone Miss Ponsonby leant over the back of her chair, reflecting. She nodded her head two or three times. "I like him," she said. "And I'm *very* sorry for his pain."

Meantime Eleanor Butler, once free of her enchaining world, lost no time in building for her future home. During her passage from Ireland to London she travelled with her party on the old coaching road through North Wales, and stayed for the night at an inn, in the beautiful valley of Llangollen. Being less fatigued than her companions, and having several hours at her disposal, she went out for a walk without being missed. In a few minutes she found herself on a slope of mountain adjacent to the village, and standing opposite a little old four-roomed cottage. She noted that it was strong and weather-proof, and empty and for sale with its bit of land. Returning to the village she enquired for the agent and found him nearby. The agent said the late owner was dead, but that for two years the house had stood empty. No one in the neighbourhood would rent or buy it, since ghosts had been seen and heard there. Miss Butler considered, and said she would give a hundred and eighty pounds for house and ground. The agent accepted her offer. At six o'clock the same evening, while her friends were preparing for the inn supper, the agent came to her with a lawyer, and the little house became hers. What a great lady should want with the kind of cottage, the vendors failed to imagine, but they understood that it would not be occupied immediately, and meantime undertook the care of it. The purchaser borrowed the key until next day. Early in the morning, while her friends slept, she slipped up the hillside again, and saw a glowing crimson sunrise from its window. Then the travelling lady passed on to her destination, and none of her companions knew what she had done.

Once in London, and throwing herself into

By permission of the County Studios, Monmouth

LLANGOLLEN VALLEY AND RIVER DEE

every experience and grasping every opportunity, Miss Butler renewed some old friendships, made notes about bookshops, met and fraternized with new Irish peers, received the calls of the persons of influence sent by her great-uncle the Archbishop, and dipped mind and soul into the stately music of the day. Her sophistication and aplomb, and her fluent French speech charmed several English statesmen and set them calculating the uses she might be to them behind the political scenes. She sweetened the air in many quarters by her sincerity. Everyone admired the simplicity with which she refused to play cards for more than a few shillings, not out of prejudice but because she did not choose to afford it. And she could not only talk agreeably, but could dance. Lord! how charming she was, dancing! In short, Miss Butler in the " best " English circles was a conspicuous success. And in the front, and back, and centre of her mind, such successes were less than nothing at all to her. She was dreaming of the day when she could stand with Sarah on that far away hillside and watch a crimson sunrise flood mountains and sky from a cottage door.

Eleanor's rough sketch and description of their future home, and the news that it was already actually their own brought joy to the lonely Sarah. In her letters she assured her friend that she was happy and begged her not to cut short the interesting time she was having in London. Eleanor wrote that their great difficulty would be in managing their first break with their friends. Over that they must take time and pains, for nothing would prevent their plan from causing both a social and family uproar when they came to executing it. When that time arrived they must be as clever as possible.

Meantime in London Miss Butler was, in her chaperon's view, behaving with criminal un-reason. She appeared to be giving no heed whatever to the purpose with which she had been sent south. A year had passed and Lady Hartskill had no engagement to report to her parents. But one morning, when they were sitting at home together, Lady Hartskill raised her eyes from her embroidery and said :

" I suppose you have heard from the Earl of Kilbriggin, Eleanor ? "

Her companion laughed. " I suppose *you* have also."

" Yes, he tells me he wishes to pay his addresses to you—desires to make you his wife."

" He asks me for an interview."

" What are you going to say ? "

" I have already written that my engagements will not permit me to see him—that I am shortly returning to Ireland."

" Oh, my dear! One of the most powerful and popular of the new Irish lords ! "

" What has that to do with me ? I am not a Member of Parliament."

" No, but think what he could do for your father! "

" Let him do it for my father then."

" He might do it more thoroughly for you."

" He will never do that."

" Why ? Don't you want it ? "

" Yes, but I shall not ask for it."

" Why not, Eleanor ? "

" When a woman asks for favours she puts a price on them. I am not selling anything."

" That is perfectly ridiculous, Eleanor. He admires you enormously, and as he is going to live in Ireland of course you are the right woman for him. Don't you know your value ? "

" Love cannot be assessed in any terms but its own."

" There you are too deep for me, my dear. I don't know what that means."

" Love is its own reward."

" You are thinking of virtue are you not . . . and I never could see——"

" Nor I, but virtue is not love. It is one of its antidotes. Lady Hartskill, I am teasing you, when what you want to know is how you shall answer that letter to yourself. Say, if you please, that I will not see him on any account, nor must the subject be referred to again. Put that as sweetly, as gracefully as you like, but no less."

Lady Hartskill began to shed tears of exasperation and disappointment. It seemed that she would get nothing out of this affair for herself.

" Add, if you like, that my affections are already engaged."

" Then you would be challenged for the name."

" Oh no! That's my own affair. But, à la bonne heure! I'm sorry indeed to be such a plague, but it will soon be over. Forgive me, won't you ? You have been so good."

The next day Miss Butler went out riding early, and later in the morning Lady Hartskill received Lord Kilbriggin. It is due to her to say that she supported Miss Butler well and put forward her meaning to perfection.

" I have conveyed the whole substance of your proposal to Miss Butler, my lord, and I regret to tell you that she rejects it. Rejects it, too, with an emphasis that leaves no doubt in my mind that it is entirely distasteful to her."

" Have you conveyed to her my request that I may have an interview with her ? "

" I have, but she sees no advantage in that. Miss Butler, as you know, is a mature woman of the world and not an easily-influenced girl. Her refusal is less uncivil than it might be in one much younger. It is really to be interpreted as a definite intimation of intentions which cannot be modified, and to state which in person might only cause you pain which she is unwilling to inflict. Her heart should receive the credit."

" But this reply is confounding, my lady. No woman could have been more gracious and charming to me. All through the season I have met her, and owing to her eloquent discourse and fine manner have decided that she is a woman of sound judgment, and a most fitting discreet head for my household. She is of such abounding health, she would give a man the finest children. My lady, she is the one woman I desire. Could she have been as affable as she has been to me and now refuse to see me ? "

" I am afraid she could, my lord. Miss Butler is no coquette. Nowhere would you hear that of her. But her agreeable and friendly manner is the same to everyone. No man should argue from that any preference for himself."

" Would you not do me the favour to open the subject to her once more, conveying to her that I take it ill that she will not speak with me ? "

"My lord, I cannot do it. She has expressly forbidden me."

"Should I write to her again?"

"That would be as you choose. It could not advantage you."

The Earl sat considering, and then said, "You tell me there is no other gentleman in her mind?"

Lady Hartskill hesitated. "Not that I know of . . . but . . . really I do not know." She was silent for a space and then added, "If I may presume to advise you, you should see Mr. Butler, her father."

"Er . . . the family do not need money?"

"Oh no! They are well off. Miss Butler will have £10,000 on her marriage. But I may tell you, Lord Kilbriggin, in confidence of course, that the family are intensely desirous of having the Ormonde peerage restored. That is much more to them than money. Miss Butler herself would welcome it. If you have influence in that direction it might carry you far."

"You may tell her I'll canvass personally every peer in the House."

"No, no. She is very proud and would regard that as a bribe. Don't speak to her. Speak to her father and get something done before you approach her again. But remember . . . I fear . . . I don't know, but I suspect . . . you have a rival somewhere——"

The door opened suddenly and Miss Butler came in, her gloves and riding-whip in her hand.

"Why, Lord Kilbriggin," she said, "I did not expect to find you here. How do you do."

Lady Hartskill slipped out of the room. Lord Kilbriggin, highly pleased at this fortunate accidental encounter, met her with a gallant smile.

" How do you do! I see, Miss Butler, that you have been taking the air on horseback. You make a fine picture for the town with your lovely colour and your eyes sparkling like stars in a frost."

Miss Butler laughed. " You might be a real Irishman, Lord Kilbriggin! You have the poetic fancy and flattering tongue."

" That should please you, Miss Butler. I hear you are returning to the old country."

" I don't think well of the Irish."

" Perhaps you are in love with the country itself. A fine setting for ladies like you, old Ireland."

" No, God forgive it for its dullness. I like England that keeps its head on its shoulders, and guns and pistols out of its hands. Ireland is not fit to live in."

Watching her glowing face and frank smile Lord Kilbriggin took a leap to his opportunity— and his doom.

" Miss Butler," he said, " er . . . Miss Butler, I am aware that when you came in here you did not know you would find me. I have therefore . . . refrained . . . from repeating the request I have already made to you . . . for a special interview . . . fearing——"

Miss Butler interrupted him deftly. " That was exceedingly considerate of you, Lord Kilbriggin, and marks you in my friendly esteem. I must thank you. We ladies are accustomed to knowing what is best in such matters. As I must change my habit, you will excuse me if I retire ? "

She rang the bell. " As we are unlikely to meet again while I am in London, I will say good-bye, begging you to convey my polite regards to your charming mother. Good-bye." She shook hands. " James, attend to Lord Kilbriggin, please." She went out of the room by another door.

Lord Kilbriggin crossed the road and entered the open ground before him with stiffened shoulders and walked with staring eyes on the ground. But soon he raised his head and spoke towards the sky.

" By God's wounds I won't take no. She's the one woman. She little knows me if she thinks I won't get her. By God, I will. If there's another fellow, pooh. I'll wipe him out! "

It may be inferred from this mingling of mortification with boasting that Lord Kilbriggin was retiring in an unpleasant temper. He was a man who was usually diligent in getting what he wanted by hook or by crook, but as a dogged hunter of fair women he had never had much success. And Miss Butler had eliminated him from her consideration as easily and effectively as Miss Ponsonby in Kilkenny was eliminating her Irish lovers.

A tiresome pair—giving great annoyance and trouble to their relatives—were these two young women, and all their friends were wondering what they should do with them next. They could not be allowed to persist indefinitely in this defiance and repudiation of their proper destiny.

CHAPTER IV

THE ROTUNDA BALL

Two flower enfolding crystal vases she
I love fills daily, mindful but of one :
And close behind pale morn she, like the sun
Priming our world with light, pours, sweet to see,
Clear water in the cup, and into me
The image of herself; and that being done,
Choice of what blooms round her fair garden run
In climbers or in creepers or the tree
She ranges with unerring fingers fine
To harmony so vivid that through sight
I hear, I have her heavenliness to fold
Beyond the senses, where such love as mine,
Such grace as hers, should the strange Fates withhold
Their starry move from her and me, unite.
                                        George Meredith.

NEXT morning Eleanor received a fat letter from
Sarah. At the moment, she was dressing, but
she dropped into a chair and opened it. " My
dear Sally," she said, " you have been keeping
something from me for some time, now you are
being good and are going to tell me all about it."
In the letter she read of Lady Betty's exhortations
to Sarah, and something about the bruising of
Sarah's ideals; she read of the rejection of
Captain Moriarty (imagine that common young
man presuming!); of Lady Betty's evident disappointment with Sarah, and of Sarah's feeling

that on account of Lady Betty—who seemed to be tired and unwell—she ought not to burden Woodstock much longer with her presence; and finally (What! Great Heaven! O Mother of God! Sally! Oh! . . . oh! . . .), yes, finally, that Sir William Fownes for several weeks past had pursued her with odious advances, and in spite of her written threat to leave his house, or tell his wife and daughter, had refused to desist from his insulting conduct. She was having to keep away from him, and Lady Betty had remarked her avoidance, and had asked her to be more pleasant to him. Her one fear was that Lady Betty might hear of his outrageous behaviour, and the problem would be how to go away and yet spare her the heartbreaking discovery. If she, Sarah, were to tell any family friend or relative, a blaze might result, and a family inquisition of the same magnitude as the one which had happened over Lady Betty's daughter. Lady Betty would never be able to stand, now, a still more dreadful occurrence. If, in the end, as was possible, the facts were discovered by others, she might be called upon to defend herself as co-offender, and might not succeed. She had, therefore, decided to tell Mrs. Goddard,* so that she might have one witness and defender. "And not a particularly good defender," commented Miss Butler, "she sits on too many fences to be that."

Sarah went on to suggest that Eleanor should return in time for the Rotunda Ball for which she would, of course, have an invitation. After that they could make plans and go away together.

* See page 276.

It seemed to her that it would be best that they should go away first, and write their explanations afterwards, or they might not succeed in getting away at all. This would probably hurt Lady Betty less, in the end, than any other course.

Eleanor Butler raised a stern flushed face after reading Sarah's letter. She thrust the letter into her dress and completed her toilet. As she went down to breakfast she told herself that Sarah was right. There were only three weeks to spare before the Dublin ball, and she must make her plans at once. After breakfast she went and sat in the room where her hostess was busy with her embroidery.

" Do you know, Eleanor, I should not be surprised if Lord Kilbriggin were to go to Ireland to see your father. From a note which I have received from him to-day he seems not disposed to give you up after one rebuff. I am sorry for him. He is entirely estimable, and very much in love with you."

" Ah! ' In love! ' What does Lord Kilbriggin know about me ? I shall be sorry if he gives himself any more unnecessary pain. However, I dare say that a conversation with my parents will help him to see the position in its true proportions."

Eleanor Butler guessed correctly that Lady Hartskill had already written to her father. Lady Hartskill regretted that she had advised Lord Kilbriggin to go to Mr. Butler, since Eleanor in her obduracy seemed to think that the meeting would only be an advantage to herself.

" Will not your parents be vexed with you ? "

" They will. I expect there will be ' wigs on the green.' May I ask you, Lady Hartskill, when you think of going to Ireland yourself ? "

" I am prepared to stay in London as long as you wish."

" To-day I have some news from a friend which makes me feel I ought to go back home."

" Well then, I will confess that I should like to chaperon my niece from Thomastown at the Rotunda Ball next month."

" Then may I not go with you ? And would you not chaperon me too, unless, of course, my parents are present."

Lady Hartskill was very much pleased with the plan. She thought it probable that both Lord Kilbriggin and Mr. Butler would be at the Dublin ball. If all were to meet there in controlling publicity, it might do a great deal to soften the atmosphere in which the Prodigal Daughter, after wasting time, beauty, and the masculine emotions of certain persons on empty air, was returning home.

Eleanor said, " I have not had a new dress for some time. I feel called on to make a special display. I think of going to Madame Ruth and ordering a dress from Paris. It will be ' positively my last appearance ' you know."

" My dear Eleanor, you alarm me! Are you contemplating a runaway match with some gentleman ? "

" Oh! I am only quoting from the play-bills. I am going to enjoy myself by making a lawful sensation in a fine frock."

They went to the shop together, and the clever little manager, Madame Ruth, was delighted with the handsome sympathetic Irish lady, who spoke perfect French, and touched her heart of an exile. While the dresses which had just arrived were being unpacked, she mopped her eyes and told Miss Butler how beautiful her little girl had looked in her first Communion frock and Miss Butler translated the story for her friend. Then, as Lady Hartskill had just decided that she too must be outfitted, the first attention was given to her needs. Eleanor picked out for her a gown of pale grey satin. " With your white hair, old lace, and diamonds —or old French jewels—don't you think ? " and her companion expressed herself as entirely pleased. " Your taste is really wonderful, my dear."

Then Madame selected for Miss Butler a narrow ivory gown, with an almost imperceptible overdress of crystal diamenté hanging from the shoulders, and with a bold touch of black on breast and shoulder.

Her chaperon demurred . . . the black . . . " Heavy ? *Mais non.* Madame would see that in a brilliantly lighted room the black would only operate *comme un couteau,* would cut out the wearer from her surroundings without violence. It was a dress for a personality . . . of distinction . . . unique. Two more suitable dresses than these could not enter an assembly together."

Lady Hartskill was requested to go to the shop next door and buy slippers of silver, pale grey, or very pale gold. In her absence Eleanor chose a beautiful half-finished model gown for Sarah of the palest rose imaginable, and she bought long creamy gloves and an upright feather ornament for Sarah's hair. She paid for the dresses, and ordered the things for Ireland to be sent off at once, for it would be a week or ten days before they were received. She enclosed a card, " For the wild-rose—My Sally."

After returning home with Lady Hartskill, Eleanor wrote her letters—first one to her parents explaining her plans and telling them that she would return again to London if they wished her to do so; then one to Sarah. It may be as well to draw a veil over Eleanor's observations in this letter, perhaps such a flower as a wild rose ought not to have heard such words, nor had the writer ever previously conceived that she could use them. They were good Shakesperian, as well as eighteenth-century names for Sarah's guardians, and might shock us more than they shocked Sarah, which was not at all. Eleanor wrote, further, that they would of course go away from Ireland immediately after the Rotunda Ball— say a week after. No, they would do nothing that they could help to pain dear Lady Betty, whom Sarah loved. She should remember her pride and pleasure in Sally's loveliness at the coming ball. And what was more, they would leave Irish Society something by which to remember them! It might be that they could arrange for Sarah to join her afterwards in London.

The period was one of great variety in dress both for men and for women. The more paltry and exaggerated French designs crossed the Channel most easily. Women's dress was usually excessive, overtrimmed and ill cut. Orgiastic Ireland liked its colours hot and crude and had little appreciation of line or form. Its handsomest men and most beautiful women had often but poor personal taste. It was certain that débutantes would be in unbecoming paper-white, and

F

others in every shade of blue, pink, green, amber, and that some of the elder women who attended would be in rich gowns made colourless by too many colours, brocades so cut up as to show no pattern, wearing hair dressed too high —or the wrong jewels.

Empire styles had not arrived, but in reaction from overpowering absurdity they were already conceived, and presently going to be born— they were already hinted at in the most select Paris models. The simple untrammelled sheath, reserving and revealing, that was Sarah's frock, pioneered another style than the one then current, and could not fail to interest Dublin. There would be many ladies in Dublin for the ball, with fine dresses from London, but the clock of London was always a little behind the Paris clock. Only clever little women like Madame Ruth knew the psychological moment for producing the new and telling thing, and only the entirely unselfconscious could wear it with grace. Lady Betty, admiring the beautiful frock, had to admit that Ireland could not have produced it.

Sarah has been asked to bring a party of four to the ball to dance a reel in green Irish peasant costume, and busied herself in getting the necessary things for Eleanor and herself, and arranging with their men partners.

The Dublin ball was a private entertainment, given, in the month of March, by four ladies. It was exclusive, and crowded with the sons and daughters and friends of great families. Ponsonbys, Butlers, Bessboroughs, Fitzgeralds, Cavendishes were there, foreign personages and their ladies, distinguished soldiers and statesmen. Young Mr. Grattan was there, and Mr. Burke and Mr. Flood. It was more or less a great tribal gathering, and upstarts such as young Captain Moriarty, in spite of his money and his dancing, had no summons to attend it. A small army of the private servants of the guests hovered in the background, many charged with the task of bringing their masters safely home in the small hours. As the guests streamed into the halls and reception rooms, the scene was brilliant. Everywhere was discipline, ceremony, fine address. Personal greetings of friends were conducted in a manner so subdued that the atmosphere seemed almost religious—only by degrees did tinkles of laughter, or the hum of conversation, break through the initial stiffness. The stream of guests advanced in good order to be announced to their hosts.

Miss Butler and Miss Ponsonby met one another, for the first time since their parting, face to face in an eddy of this flowing tide. Lady Betty had arrived, but being suddenly indisposed was resting behind the scenes; and Sarah, looking like a splendid delicate flower, was moving forward, upright in her beautiful dress, her shining coiffure and her mother's pearls, her reluctant hand upon Sir William Fownes's arm. The two friends took one short, grave look at one another, bowed, and passed on. A Butler was a Butler, and a Ponsonby was a Ponsonby— hearts might throb, but *noblesse oblige.*

After this meeting, for two hours Eleanor Butler was inwardly as one in a dream, outwardly an effective, sparkling, automaton. She met and greeted her parents, who smiled their admiration, and bade her stay with Lady Hartskill. She met and shook hands with Lord Kilbriggin, to the evident relief of that gentleman, who did not otherwise approach her during the evening. She danced with old friends, and new London acquaintances, and with some very agreeable foreign men. She failed to give a very much larger number of men any opportunities at all because there were too many of them and it was impossible. She appeared to be totally unaware that she was a special object of scrutiny, that lorgnettes were raised whenever she passed the spectators, and that the French guests, when they spoke the words *chic, distinguée,* or *haut ton,* were describing what pertained to herself. As she did her part in minuet, quadrille, and other dances, she knew that time was standing still for two persons in these rooms, although it fled by all the other guests. Her ears were open for praise of Sarah, and she gathered it up with joy.

For a few moments a group of young friends captured Sarah Ponsonby. " Sarah," said Margaret Hill, " what a simply ravishing dress you are wearing ; we are all feeling blue with envy. Tell us—everyone wants to hear—is it latest London fashion ? "

"From Paris, my dear Margaret. You like it?"

" It is wonderful! And Miss Butler's—is her's from Paris, too ? "

" I do not know. I have not seen Miss Butler for a long time. She only arrived from London this week, I believe."

" Her dress is very fine . . . but . . . is it not an *adventurous* style ? "

" Well, you know, it is an adventurous world we are in."

" We others don't get much adventure."

Sarah laughed. " It may be better, and must be more comfortable, to be good, rather than adventurous."

" Oh! I don't know . . . we don't know, do we, girls ? "

" I am sure you are all in the right fashion."

" Oh! what is the good of that. I sometimes think a false step into the world is better than no step."

" Then carry it out. Make it real. But for God's sake do not tell anyone of your intention."

Miss Ponsonby could not possibly mean what she was saying. The group laughed and dispersed.

Lord Kilbriggin, having detached himself from a prolonged interview with Mr. and Mrs. Butler, wandered about until he discovered his old friend, Sir James Mackellow. Sir James was seated where he could see Miss Butler, who was dancing a minuet. He pulled a chair forward for his friend, but the latter backed away to the wall, and beckoned him to stand with him there.

" Oho! Kilbriggin! What's the matter ? "

" Nothing. You can see from here ? "

" Yes. I'm watching the lady. She's the sincerest creature alive, but look at this little play she is acting, for fun, with her partner. No dance lends itself to coquetry like the minuet. The advance, the retreat, the half-turn, the curtsy, the pirouette, the smiles, the glances. That woman has it all at her confident disposal, oh! charming! She looks over the edge of her fan. She laughs behind it. And how striking is that black-and-cream dress. What a head of a man's house she would have made!"

"*Would have made?* It is surprising that she is not married!"

"She never will be. I can assure you that there are here to-night three men (one in that very dance) whom she has refused. How do I know? Because that prating old Butler has said so."

"I wish I knew some way of commending myself to her," said Lord Kilbriggin.

Sir James turned and looked at him. "Ha! So you are at least number four. As I know you have not tried to dance with her this evening, I presume the worst has befallen *you*."

"In confidence, yes. But her father will speak to her again——"

"Don't do it, Kilbriggin. Don't allow it. The girl has already been made sick by the pressure put on her. It's a persecution. Withdraw from that, and go and look for a nice girl whom you have some chance of understanding."

"Understanding!"

"Yes. What do *you* know about *her*? Nothing. You've never tried to know her. She is Ireland . . . you're . . . only an Irish peer. She's an artist—you're not. She's a reader, and a person of ideas; you're neither. You like hunting animals; she abhors it. She wants a companion; you haven't a tail-feather of anything to give her. She is alive; you're dead. Without knowing a thing about her, you have the impertinence to go and tell her you love her. Bah! Father! Bah!"

Deeply disturbed, as his errors dawned upon him, Lord Kilbriggin said he would think it over from Sir James' point of view.

About half past ten the supper rooms began to fill, and at eleven o'clock Eleanor, who was peacefully engaged in shattering the heart of an elderly Frenchman, was called upstairs to change her dress for the reel. Sarah was already in the dressing-room with the maid from Woodstock, Mary Carryl. After Eleanor entered, Mary Carryl closed the door and turned the key, and smiled benignly upon the two friends as, walking in silence towards one another, they embraced.

" Sure Miss Butler," Mary said, " the sight of you is a cure for sore eyes, and everyone admiring you, but before all, ma'am, 'tis Miss Sarah that has need of you—the flower that she is! "

" I know, Mary." Miss Butler stopped kissing Sarah for a moment and looked round to smile. " I'll make all well for her! "

" Mind you, her dress, ma'am, she mustn't drop tears on it. Let me take the things off of yez, the way ye can kiss in peace."

" But we must change at once, Eleanor. Shoes and stockings first, Mary."

They hurriedly took off their dresses and put on the peasant costumes.

" How is it all going, Sarah ? I seem to be dazed."

" Oh, it's a lovely ball—everyone is happy."

" Splendid! How comfortable these shoes are. We must dance like . . . like——"

" Yes! and talk when we come upstairs afterwards. Eleanor! Heart of my heart! I could kiss you for a year."

" They're coming to fetch yez. Come away, ma'am."

Separating them, Mary Carryl thrust Eleanor's

green skirt over her head, and fastened it. " Now
the white vest. Now the jacket, and let me see
that your stockings is on straight, and your shoes
fastened well. Now you, Miss Sarah; and pass
the comb through your hair. There now, ma'am!
God bless the dance. The servants is wild to see
it."

Their two young partners, Sir George Gresson
and Mr. Carmichael, stood in their green stockings and breeches and white shirts and green
jackets waiting for them in a group of young men
at the foot of the staircase. Lorgnettes were fixed
all round the hall as the two friends descended,
holding each other's gloveless hands, faces turned
towards one another, flushed, radiant, happy,
with the lights pouring on their vivid clothing.

" Regarde-moi des ingénues," said a French
marquise. " Et après, nous attendons quelque
chose la plus endiablée, n'est-ce-pas ? "

The band struck up a swift medley of reels and
most of the company followed the four performers
to the ballroom. Others occupied rows of chairs
in the large open doorways or stood farther back,
while the crowd of servants crept on to the gallery
or half-way down the staircase.

As they gained the centre of the floor Miss
Butler said to her companions, " We are not in a
ballroom, we are out in the woods under the
moon, and doing this for our own enjoyment! "

" A true word, Miss Butler. We are not men
at all, but just fairy-folks."

" And we'll bring the woods into the room,
Miss Butler."

The ignorant among the spectators, whose
conception of an Irish reel was a clumsy folk-

dance in which the time was kept by the beat of heavy boots on the floor, received a surprise. The roll of a light drum started the band and the dance was taken at a full speed. The drum marked the time, and the light feet of the dancers were not heard. But their rhythmic touches on the floor, the essence of such a dance, were perfect. Their lightness and grace were perfect. The poised arms with outstretched fingers, the leaps, the quick rapturous turns together were entrancing. The youth and joy of the dancers affected both old and young, and soon these green creatures from the woods seemed to be bringing the world of Nature indoors. The spirit that moved them was not the bacchanalian spirit of harvest time, but rather that of rushing streams and fertilizing winds, the spirit that blows where it lists, the spirit of freedom—the wind that had blown through Tara's halls, and through the souls of all Irish people. Even Mrs. Goddard, who—creaking somnolently in maroon velvet and a golden turban, and replete with wine and supper—was watching the dancers, felt the mystery breeze that blew through the hot room. Some of the servants, who knew that green fairy-folk could transport a soul elsewhere and lose it before its time, crossed themselves as they felt it. But Mr. and Mrs. Butler, Lord Kilbriggin and Sir William Fownes, felt no wind of the spirit, and only experienced an access of their own anguished greed. These dancing sprites were no relatives of theirs.

The dance was not very long, and when it stopped there was a complete silence for a moment, and then polite society burst its bonds, and broke into clapping and loud cheering. The pleased hosts hastened to congratulate and thank the dancers, when loud cries of " encore " arose, and after a short rest the haunting magic music struck up again.

" This time," suggested Miss Ponsonby, " let us dance for freedom—over the hills and far away."

" Ireland," assented the two young men, and the second dance went forward with a spirit that surpassed the first. In the loud applause that followed there were shouts of " Ireland!" and " Freedom! "

It would not do to rouse the sleeping orgiast in this place, and the performers moved away at once. People crowded round them as they went, and touched the green dresses as though there was magic in the colour. At last the two ladies, breaking through the crowd, ran lightly up the stairs and disappeared. In half an hour they appeared again, smart, dignified, correct, each carrying a beautiful bouquet; and the ball continued.

Next day, Miss Ponsonby went back to Woodstock and Miss Butler went back to Kilkenny Castle. Before the latter arrived at her home, a letter had reached Mr. Butler from Lord Kilbriggin, saying that as he had reflected that a renewal of his suit could only be annoying or painful to Miss Butler, he begged to withdraw his intention of appealing to her again.

After her return home, Eleanor, realizing with what mixed emotions her parents must have regarded her success at the ball, replied as pleasantly as she could to all Mrs. Butler's

By permission of Messrs. Fox, Greenhough & Company, Kilkenny

KILKENNY CASTLE—ANOTHER VIEW

questions about her dancing partners, and about her life in London. On her second day at home she noted that a letter lying on her father's desk had come from Lord Kilbriggin. Her parents said nothing to her, but they were evidently mortified by its contents. In the evening, when alone with them, she risked starting a conversation on her own account, always a perilous thing to do.

Addressing her mother she said, " My London visit has been exceedingly enjoyable. I have made some good friends and improved my knowledge of the world, and other things."

" Then I hope you have changed your ideas."

" If you mean about marriage, I am sorry to disappoint you. I am of the same mind. I had two offers of marriage, about one of which I see you know—Lord Kilbriggin. I recognized his handwriting on your table to-day. I gave no man any encouragement as that would not have been fair. I want now to consider my future with you."

" What future ? You haven't a future at this rate. Your family is not going to be made ridiculous by your eccentricity. Enjoying yourself as you did at the Dublin ball! Three letters to your father! Nothing to come of them! It can't go on."

" I agree. I do not think I ought to stay at home. I am willing to go back to England, and shall easily make for myself a happy life. That will really be best."

" The best thing for you is a convent; you can't make scandals there."

" Oh, yes, I could. In France you can make

them easily—if you want to. But I shall not
consent to go to a convent. I am not the kind of
woman who is to be found in those places. I
must have my liberty. I shall never abuse it. I
shall always live as a Butler and a lady should.
If you give me the money you would pay to a
convent for keeping me, I can manage to live
on that."

It may be remarked that the French convents
did not take recalcitrant ladies, liable to flee
away over walls, for nothing.

" The money would not buy you those smart
dresses."

" No, I would of course like to have a sufficient
income to be able to maintain my social position.
But the power to secure in what manner I live
is with you—my parents."

" And if your father and I do not agree to this
scheme ? "

" I hope you will consider that my life here is
intolerable. If I am at a distance we shall be all
the better friends. I should come back to you
sometimes, of course."

" Behave like a disreputable bachelor ? "

" No. I am always respected."

She looked over at her father. " If you enable
me to do what I want, it will be better for me to
do it at once, before our neighbours know that
I am back from London. They will think nothing
of my being away——"

" Your mother must decide——"

" I say No. She is ashamed of her parents, I
suppose ! "

" Well, your mother says No. Let us hear no
more about it."

There was no other occasion for some time when it would have been profitable to lead Mr. Butler back to the subject. He had relapsed into a period of invalidism. Eleanor made one more attempt to speak to each of her parents separately on the subject, but they would not hear her. She was to be punished for their disappointment.

Chapter V

FIRST FLIGHT

Ah! Let us make no claim
On life's incognisable sea
To too exact a steering of our way!
Let us not fret and fear to miss our aim
If some fair coast has lured us to make stay,
Or some friend hailed us to keep company.

. . . . .

Even so we leave behind,
As, charter'd by some unknown Powers,
We steer across the sea of life by night,
The joys which were not for our use design'd
The friends to whom we had no natural right
The homes that were not destined to be ours.
Matthew Arnold.

THE Dublin ball, in spite of its exclusive and private nature, eventually had every kind of public attention drawn to it. After it was over, from a fine entertainment it became enlarged into a very important occurrence, and descriptions of it, chiefly unauthorized, and eulogies of all the beauty and charm it had contained, grew as they circulated. By no means all of the rank and fashion of Southern Ireland had been there, yet to have been there was something to boast about, while not to have been there was, for some families, to have suffered loss or a certain degree of social eclipse.

94

In dancing the reel Miss Butler and Miss Ponsonby had only undertaken to do in all simplicity what they knew they could do efficiently and what the white-paper débutantes or more experienced dancers had been too diffident to attempt. But they had created a flutter in many Irish homes. They had said they would give Ireland something to remember them by and they had done it. In a country in which the making of advantageous matrimonial alliances was of every importance, the appearance of their sons and daughters at so brilliant an affair as the Dublin ball caused maternal hearts to beat, and paternal pride to swell.

When congratulations came to Sir William Fownes upon the charm of his young relative Miss Ponsonby, he beamed and took them as to his personal credit. Lady Betty, her complacency somewhat restored, returned to Woodstock hoping afresh that her pretty Sally would now capitulate to some insistent lover, since obviously, whether she would or no, she had disturbed the peace of several fine young men. As to the handsome Miss Butler, with her quiet challenging air to one man, her earnest interest in another, her wholesome laughter with a third, her frank enjoyment with all men, she had handed round a heady sparkling beverage in a golden cup of expectation. And yet all those who had tasted it had found themselves next day left to the torments of unrealizable dreams.

In the drawing-rooms of a hundred great houses, in clubs, and hunting-boxes, and barracks, conjectures born of small incidents abounded, reminiscences and comparisons flowed, titles were appraised, incomes and dowries were calculated, not least by the young ladies and young gentlemen who were as yet unwed. Miss Ponsonby's circumstances were not generally known, but it was not to be supposed that a young woman with so many rich relatives would not bring money to a " good " marriage. Miss Butler, difficult as she was proving to capture, would assuredly come to her chosen husband well endowed with money.

Envious tongues were not wanting, for there were men who had expressed themselves freely in their homes on the subject of the Ponsonby-Butler standards of good taste and refinement, as seen at the Dublin ball. In a time when both men and women took fewer baths than the succeeding generations, but used powder, rouge, and somewhat flagrant perfumes, the Ponsonby-Butler standard was delicately clean, and free from all doubtful aids to personal effect. Even the French marquise who had dubbed them sarcastically as " *ingénues*," and whose own daughter had been a monument of skilful paint and gilding and creamy colour washes, had realized the superiority of lovely Irish complexions untouched by art. After the ball, a flow of critical correspondence or of expressions of un-selfish admiration, or of willingness to follow the lead of the two pioneers of fashion, circulated among the ladies of Ireland, and expectation of news to follow ran high.

Under such circumstances a shock sustained by high society must of necessity be severe. Society was awaiting events, but not the event which was to come.

Meantime, Sarah was becoming more and more anxious and unhappy, and was running a certain grave risk to her character. She wrote that she believed the Woodstock servants, especially Mary Carryl, must be noticing things. She thought they had better not wait longer, and would therefore make all necessary preparations for going away and would give Eleanor the signal when and where to meet her.

The only person who knew that Miss Ponsonby's little store of personal property was being overhauled and some of it packed, was Mary Carryl, the maid who attended to her room. And Mary had observed more than this. She had noticed that Miss Ponsonby refused to go for walks with Sir William, but went out at times, and at unusual hours, alone. She noted that for her own part Miss Ponsonby avoided Sir William in the house, and spoke shortly to him, and that for his part he pursued her with looks of admiration and with small attentions, was solicitous for her pleasure and evidently desired more of her company than he could obtain.

Mary's mind was already filled with the suspicion that all was not going well, and when she sensed the preparations made by Miss Ponsonby she felt sure that a secret flight was intended. A daily stream of letters were now passing to and from Kilkenny Castle, and recalling the demonstration she had witnessed in the dressing-room on the night of the ball, she felt sure that if Miss Ponsonby were about to do anything without the knowledge of her hosts Miss Butler would be a party to it.

G

At last she ventured to speak to Miss Ponsonby.

" 'Tis a hard case that you don't see more of Miss Butler, ma'am, the friends that ye are, and the two of yez made for one another."

Miss Ponsonby turned calmly, and looked the speaker in the face.

" Mary—if you want to be our friend, will you take care—if anything should happen to me, to know nothing whatever about it."

(" Our friend! " Thank God——)

Mary replied, " I'd go in chains for you two ladies."

" Meantime, until we ask you, know nothing, see nothing, say nothing."

Mary Carryl heaved a great sigh. "I'll go through fire but I'll do what you ask, ma'am."

" Your opportunity may come for serving us better than that."

" May God send it, ma'am."

And when two days later on calling Miss Ponsonby in the morning, she found her bed unslept in, a window wide open and the bird flown, she raised no alarm. However, Sarah was missed at breakfast time. It was thought that, as the morning was so fine, she might be in the gardens; but when sought, she was not found there, and when Sir William and Lady Betty had finished breakfast, her absence and the fact of the open window were reported to them.

Then Sir William knew that she had fulfilled her threat and run away from Woodstock, and suddenly he became a prey to guilty panic. He must find her, and reassure her with promises. She might have run away, and she had told him that for his wife's sake she would not betray him;

but something else might do so. While he was giving orders for a wide search, and Lady Betty was standing at his side shedding tears, a coach drove up to the door and Mr. Butler alighted. Apologizing for the hour of his call, he said that his daughter had been missing from her home since the evening before, and it had occurred to them that she might have come to Woodstock to see Miss Ponsonby. They did not otherwise know what to think of her disappearance.

Lady Betty and Sir William both exclaimed, " Then they have gone away together."

" What? Miss Ponsonby is missing too? "

" Yes, and no time must be lost in overtaking them. The Waterford road——" Servants were sent from both houses in all directions in search of the fugitives.

When the time for her escape from Woodstock House had come, Sarah could not risk making the noise that unbolting the main door would have occasioned, so she quietly opened a low window, and dropped into a flower-bed beneath. She went down to the gates and there, by a previous arrangement, a labouring man with a lantern met her, and they set out in the dark for a long walk. The trysting place was a large barn off the main road to Waterford, but close to a village, and when they arrived Eleanor had already reached the spot. Eleanor asked Sarah's guide where they could obtain a car. They were told close at hand. " Let you not go forward to-morrow, my lady, they'll all be hunting your honours to-morrow. Let the chase get past you. When it falls dark to-morrow, pick up the car. They'll take you to Waterford for the money, even if afterwards they tell on you. But you should be there for the rising of the sun, and why wouldn't you get away safely ? "

" We are much obliged to you." Eleanor gave him a gold piece.

" Sure I've been young meself, ma'am. Fine young ladies like yourselves is bound to meet good fortune."

" You're quite sure you won't let anyone screw the truth out of you ? "

" Divvle a truth, lady, and God help the lie. 'Tis my wife will be telling that, and me knowing nothing at all but snoring by her side this whole night."

He lifted several trusses of hay to a corner behind the barn door, showed them how to fasten the door inside, and departed.

The night was silent, except that a pair of owls hooted and shuffled in the roof. Dawn was breaking, and faint streaks of light were showing through holes in the boards of the barn.

They made a warm hollow in the hay and slipped down in it to sleep.

" Prayers first, Sally. Let us rest in the name of the Father, and of the Son and of the Holy Ghost, Amen."

" Mavourneen! " and in another minute Sarah, exhausted by her long tramp, was asleep with her head on Eleanor's breast. They slept far into next day, and then rose, and ate some of the food Eleanor had brought. The hay had made a dusty bed, and Sarah appeared to have a cold.

In the evening they went in search of the car, and next morning alighted at the Ship Inn, Waterford.

But when Sarah threw back her hood Eleanor was startled to see that she was ill. She could not eat breakfast, and was flushed and shivering, owned to a swollen throat and difficulty in swallowing.

After Eleanor had looked at her throat, and felt her burning hands she said, " This has beaten us, Sally. I could not risk taking you on the sea like this. I must take you back home."

" Oh, must it be ? Must it ? "

" We know it must. When you are better we will start again, and next time we will go openly —there will be nothing else to do. Now we must face, not the sea, but the family clamour! Stay in here and I will go out and get a post-chaise or covered carriage. I will send you a little brandy and water. Try to drink it."

As Eleanor reached the door of the inn, a footman from Woodstock came towards her, touching his hat. " Lady Betty Fownes' compliments, madam. Her coach is at the side door on the left. She desires to speak with you."

Lady Betty had spent the night in Waterford, hoping to encounter the fugitives sooner or later. She was starting early to enquire about the town for them. They were found. Miss Butler came to the door of the coach, and stood in silence before Lady Betty.

" Miss Butler, where is Sarah Ponsonby ? "

" She is here, Lady Betty. She will come to you. I regret to say she is very unwell with a severe cold. We could not risk crossing the sea and I was now about to return with her. Everything shall be explained to you if you will be good enough to take us back home with you . . .

until she is better . . . I hope . . . you would not separate us . . . while she is ill."

" My dear Miss Butler, of course you shall go with us. Only bring her at once, I pray you."

A fresh complication ensued, for another carriage drew up and Mrs. Hamerton, a connection of Eleanor's, and Mr. Morton Kavanagh, her brother-in-law, got out and came to the door of Lady Betty's coach.

Mr. Kavanagh said sternly, " Eleanor, your father's orders are that you are to go with us at once."

" Why am I to go with you—and where ? "

" In the first place to our house—to Ballyhale. After that I am not sure, but your father will not receive you in his house. You are forbidden to go there. You *must* come with us."

" There is no ' must,' Mr. Kavanagh. Lady Betty will shelter me."

" Do not be silly. Do you want your father to cut you off with a shilling. Come to your sister."

Mrs. Hamerton said persuasively, " Since your father insists, do come. Come into safety, and talk it over with us."

" Lady Betty, what do you advise."

" If I were in your situation, Miss Butler, I should do what your father orders. It will be more easy for you in the end. Go with your relations, my dear; Sarah will be well cared for."

" Then will you give me time to consult Sally, and get her consent ? "

" Of course, my dear. I entreat you to hasten, Sally should travel home quickly, and be in bed."

Eleanor went back to Sarah: " Sally, Lady

Betty is here for you, and they have come for me from Ballyhale."

Sarah said nothing, but looked at Eleanor with a kind of terror in her face.

Eleanor's mind had worked swiftly. "Lady Betty says she will take me to Woodstock. But while you are in bed there, I should be in everyone's way. My people might make trouble there. It would not do. At Borris I could better arrange for our next flight. And I can parley with my father through my relations. We must bear to part, Sally, for some days. In about a week you may be better."

" I dare say you are right."

" You will consent ? "

" Yes. I must."

" Come now with me, sweetheart."

Eleanor picked up Sarah's shawl and her own cloak. To the footman who was waiting in the porch she handed Sarah's valise. She led Sarah to the coach, put her own cloak round her shoulders as an additional wrap, helped her into the coach beside Lady Betty, and spread the shawl over her knees. In their total silence Lady Betty was sensible of the pain that was beating in the air round about her. In place of anger against Miss Butler, her heart was moved to charity. This outcast daughter, defeated, punished, forbidden her home, was after all Sally's friend, the one who had come laughing down the staircase at the Dublin ball hand in hand with her—who had danced so beautifully with her— who had delighted everyone.

" Miss Butler, you are not forbidden my house. You shall come to Sally and Sally to you, when she is better."

Eleanor, tongue-tied, her eyes full of anguish, could only incline her head in acknowledgment of the kind speech. She stepped back on the pavement. The footman came forward and shut the door and the carriage drove away.

Sarah lay ill in bed at Woodstock with an acute tonsilitis from April 2nd to April 6th. While in the coach on the way to Woodstock she had handed Lady Betty the letter which she and Eleanor had written explaining what they had done. In the absence of the whole of the facts the letter was really as unconvincing as Lady Betty felt it to be. Although for four or five days she hardly left Sarah's bedside, conversation between them was not possible. In the long hours in which she sat, fearing with exaggerated fears for Sarah's reason, and life itself, and brooding over the extraordinary events that had happened, she was not unnaturally liable to relapse from the kindly feeling which she had shown to Miss Butler in the first moments of the submission of the captives. On reviewing the situation she was inclined to regard her poor suffering Sally as the unconscious victim of Miss Butler's seductions and odious example. She had heard from Miss Butler's relatives that they were exceedingly angry with her, that it was intended to place her in a convent in France, and as she contemplated the sad, sick girl on her hands, she hoped that some such clean cut in their association would be effected, and she expressed this hope when writing to her friend, Mrs. Goddard. Miss Butler had troubled the peace of them all. Let Miss Butler be caused to disappear. Sally might be long in getting over her escapade, but no doubt she would in the end see her folly. Girls often had to get over their youthful emotions when ordered to do so. What Sally and Miss Butler had to do, argued Lady Betty to herself, was to fall in love with the right man, spontaneously, or if not, by order, and take all the consequences that might have to be taken of doing so. That remained the duty of each. Sarah, however, broke in on Lady Betty's musings by becoming able to talk, and her condition improved quickly. Seven days after the onset of her illness she was able to write herself to Mrs. Goddard, and a little later to drive over to Borris to see her friend. She also talked about Eleanor to Lady Betty.

" Tell me, now, Sally, how long have you been so much attached to Miss Butler ? "

" Ever since I first knew her, before I came here. She has a beautiful mind. She has a fine character, and has been a good daughter to her parents. I love her for all her good qualities."

" I don't know that that explains your both leaving your friends."

" Lady Betty, you don't need to be told that I love you. You know I do, and you have been perfectly good to me. But I am young, and you are much older. I live *your* life, and always should if I stayed here. But it isn't mine. I don't care for visiting, and I don't want to marry. If I did all the things that, of my own choice, I should like to do, I should have to shut myself up alone to do them. I couldn't do that here. Eleanor and I want the same things and we could do them together."

" My dear—is there nothing else ? Have you no private trouble ? "

Lady Betty thought they might each have an unrequited attachment to some man.

" I won't tell you a lie. Yes, I have a private trouble, and Eleanor also has a quite separate private trouble of her own. We want to get clear of those, but we intend never to tell anybody what those troubles are. So you mustn't ask me."

" Well, my dear, I must see what I can do to give you more love and more happiness."

" You can do that by agreeing that I may go away. I *must* go. When Eleanor comes here for me we shall have to go. I shall leave you in sorrow, but I think it my duty. Will you remember that . . . when I . . . afterwards ? It is not a parting for good——"

Meantime Miss Butler, in her relations' temporary keeping, first at Ballyhale and then at Borris, was firmly refusing to be imprisoned in a convent. The Archbishop had a letter from Walter Butler asking him to exert his spiritual authority or influence generally over his daughter. But the Archbishop was an astute man of the world. He did not make second ventures when he realized there was no hope of success. He saw that there was an untamable human creature involved, and one whom the thunders of Holy Church could not coerce. His reply to Walter Butler was a distinct refusal to do anything. He said that those convents were *not* nice places, and not for Irish ladies like his great-niece. He had heard nothing but good of her in London, he did not despair, as her friends did, of her being married. Give her the allowance she asked for, and let her go back to London. If her young friend chose to go too, why not ? Romantic friendships were childish bagatelles—not to be regarded—they always broke up. Better than trying to do the impossible, send her to England again. That would be the best possible thing. However, before the Archbishop's advice was taken, in order to satisfy Mrs. Butler, Eleanor was offered a handsome income if she would go voluntarily and live in a convent for some years. This offer having failed, there was a lull in the affairs of each of the friends before a fresh storm broke. During the lull, on April 9th, Lady Betty and Sarah Ponsonby both wrote to Mrs. Goddard, earnestly desiring her help, Lady Betty for her help with Sarah Ponsonby, Sarah for her help with Lady Betty. But the call to come to the help of the distressed parties was unwelcome to Mrs. Goddard. It was unwelcome because she knew too much, and while she did not see of what use she could really be, she did see that in groping among powder-barrels she might inadvertently touch off a train of explosive and wreck the situation. She was not clever, and knew it. She was not, moreover, possessed of any feeling whatever for those who liked and trusted her.

The chase of the fugitives had been in itself enough to send the news of their flight all over Ireland. The important thing was to explain the flight. At once Lady Betty's daughter, Mrs. Tighe, wrote to the central news exchange, Mrs. Goddard, with the benign intention of making the least of the occurrence. " The Runaways are caught and we shall soon see our amiable friend again whose conduct, though it has the appearance of imprudence, is I am sure void of serious impropriety. There were no gentlemen concerned, nor does it appear to be anything more than a scheme of Romantic Friendship."*

Mrs. Tighe was however to hear a little later that one gentleman had been concerned whose serious improprieties had resulted in Sarah Ponsonby's flight from under his roof—and that gentleman Mrs. Tighe's own father.

On April 2nd, 4th and 5th, when Sarah's fever was daily increasing, Lady Betty wrote to Mrs. Goddard urgent requests to come to Woodstock. Mrs. Goddard received these letters on April 6th, together with news from two other friends that Sarah was seriously ill. She made no attempt to go, but went that night to the theatre.

Lady Betty's distraction was evident in her letters to Mrs. Goddard, who received her many exaggerated phrases with entire unconcern—when Mrs. Goddard exaggerated herself, which was very seldom, she knew what she was doing. Instead of making reply to Lady Betty's calls for help, she went on with her amusements, leaving the letters on her dressing-table where, after she had unskilfully applied her rouge, they were marked with red finger-marks. " God send Sally may soon come to herself," wrote Lady Betty. " . . . I am almost out of my wits." " She has raved of you." Of Miss Butler: " Many an unhappy hour she has cost me, and I am convinced years to Sally." " What I suffer you may guess." Of Sarah: " Anything against Miss Butler is death to her." " She has taken my little senses away." " If she (her daughter) had not been here I must have died I think."* " If you won't come I shall give myself up at once."

* *The Hamwood Papers.*

Mrs. Goddard treated the two letters received on the 9th in the same way and did not go to Woodstock. Some time after the 9th Sarah drove to Borris to see Eleanor. Then came the lull in which everyone awaited with anxiety the next movements of the young insurgents.

On the 20th Lady Betty received the news that Miss Butler was again missing, and her friends were searching for her. Eleanor arrived at Woodstock late on Sunday night. Not wishing to disturb the family, she managed to be admitted quietly through a window. On Monday she remained in Sarah's room discussing plans. Lady Betty found her there. At the moment when Lady Betty came into the room both friends were weeping.

" Miss Butler! I am much surprised! "

Eleanor stood up. " I certainly owe you an apology. I came away from Borris yesterday, but was so late in arriving that I could not disturb your household, and Sally let me in. Since then I have been trying to comfort poor Sally, who, as you see, is much distressed. Lady Betty, I have come for Sally, that we may go away together again."

" And I am going with Eleanor, Lady Betty. It was all arranged the day I went over to Borris."

Oh, that Mrs. Goddard were here! Lady Betty saw a chance of effecting a meeting between Sarah and Mrs. Goddard if she kept Miss Butler in the house.

" Be seated, my dear. I hope you will stay here as long as you like and give us all an opportunity of talking together. This is a rather dreadful thing for me and Sir William, you will realize that."

"Yes, and I am entirely at your service, Lady Betty. Anything I could do to soften the pain that you and Sally both feel, I am only too willing to do. Before we go, we both feel that we ought to allow everyone to say all they have to say to us. I thank you sincerely . . . if I am not in your way here——"

"You know we are not running away this time," Sarah said. "We are going perfectly openly, at your convenience and Sir William's."

"But your own family, Miss Butler——"

"There are no complications there. My parents refuse to see me."

"As your father notified us you were missing yesterday, Sir William must inform him that you are here."

"If Sir William pleases. It will make no difference to me. It grieves me most truly to be a party to the pain and inconvenience to which we have put you. I hope when this is all over that you will accept me as Sally's friend. I shall love you for her sake. Excepting for her . . . I am . . . very much . . . alone."

"I don't know that I can ever forgive or trust you, Miss Butler, since your own people do not. But meantime you are our guest. We will do our best to understand one another."

Sarah flung her arms round Lady Betty and kissed her. "Do be good to her," she whispered.

On April 24th, having been informed that Miss Butler was at Woodstock and the friends intending to leave together, and having been once more urgently summoned, Mrs. Goddard, realizing that matters were now desperate, set out for Woodstock, arriving on the 25th. It was not until two days later that she had the much desired interview with the two friends. She knew that Miss Butler knew of Sarah's great difficulty owing to Sir William's conduct. But it had apparently never occurred to herself that a young girl ought not to remain in a house in which an elderly man had lost his head on her account, and was subjecting her to a conscienceless persecution. Ignoring this crucial fact, Mrs. Goddard launched out into an address upon the duty of submission to the will of parents and guardians, " and as you have always hitherto recognized, Miss Ponsonby, you have a special duty not to annoy or hurt Lady Betty." The two friends, smiling encouragement, allowed her to talk her voluble fill. Glancing through her keen little ferret's eyes at their attentive faces, she thought she was making an excellent impression. " You see, my dears, I am able, as a woman of the world, to assure you that your project would never do, like sensible creatures make up your minds to give it up. Such a romance as yours is simply not proper, and time is passing, and you ought both to be married. Well, that is what it is my duty to say to you."

" Thank you very much, Mrs. Goddard. One question more. Do you think, in view of Sir William's conduct, that Miss Ponsonby's position here is satisfactory ? "

" Miss Ponsonby's position ? Why, she has been equal to it so far. Why should she not continue equal to it——"

" You don't think then that it furnishes a reason for her leaving this house ? "

" No. Perhaps now that I am here I can give Miss Ponsonby some advice as to how to——"

" You think," asked Sarah, interrupting her, " that I can put up with insults indefinitely, and can honourably accept the presents of money and clothing which have been provided for me here."

" Why not ? You are a relative. You give value in your companionship with Lady Betty."

" The servants here are noticing how things are. In the circumstances, is my own character safe ? "

" My dear Miss Ponsonby, whoever thinks of listening to servants, or of being afraid of them ? At a hint from you, Sir William would send them packing."

Mrs. Goddard was asked whether she thought there was such a thing as loyalty due to Lady Betty on Sarah's part, or on Sir William's.

" Your letters to Sir William show you have been most loyal. As to Sir William's loyalty— well, we are not in the garden of Paradise; we are obliged to take men as we find them."

" That obligation may account for my preference for Miss Butler and hers for me."

" Here you are back to your romantic stuff, my dear."

" I am to let myself be an occasion of Sir William's disloyalty ? "

" Nonsense. We must take men as we find them, I tell you, and overlook . . . most things. No doubt Lady Betty has her share of trouble poor dear, and here you are proposing to give

her more on your own account. Well, I have told
you what I think. Do grow into women of the
world—and learn to put a man in his proper
place."

" Tea is served, ladies."

" Coming at once, Richard." They all rose.

In order to let Mrs. Goddard go first Miss
Butler politely made way for her. But if Mrs.
Goddard could have encountered a mirror, or
have turned round suddenly, she might have
seen two grave pitying young faces turn towards
one another in mute comment on her " worldly "
advice. " Under-worldly " Eleanor afterwards
called it, and said it reeked of corruption.

Mrs. Goddard told Lady Betty that she believed
she had made an excellent impression, and had
swept a few cobwebs from before their young
friends' outlook.

And Lady Betty said, " Bless you, my dear
Lucy. We all wanted your help, and knew that
we should have it."

Next day, however, when, full of hope, Lady
Betty initiated another conversation, the stream
of Mrs. Goddard's eloquence ran dry. She failed
to impress her audience through over-caution.
Eleanor also hung back, and the conversation
devolved mainly on Lady Betty and Sarah.
Again Sarah saved the subject from too much
repetition by adroit questions, and Mrs. Goddard
found herself stammering, and admitting that
since we are all human beings under the Christian
dispensation, and called to be saints, we were
bound to take the very highest view of love and
loyalty, and of faithfulness to the sworn word.
Sarah said that this admission seemed to be in

H

conflict with the view Mrs. Goddard had expressed yesterday about taking the world as we found it, and the men in it as they were. Such a view would of course affect one's selection of a partner in marriage.

Mrs. Goddard was flustered. Impersonal discussions were not her strong suit, and she retired in disorder. This was impish of Sarah, but Mrs. Goddard had asked for it.

But Lady Betty laughed, and said that *of course* we must aim at the highest.

Sarah asked, " Would you say that we must accept anything less ? "

" No, my dear. God does not give us commands which we are not able to carry out. But we are responsible for what we choose."

" That is what Eleanor and I believe. We have been so much astonished that the men who proposed to us, as well as our friends who encouraged them, have never cared to tell us about themselves, and their ideas, or whether they had any principles of their own. Nor did they care what ours were. Just a few preliminaries about money or family, and that was enough."

" All the rest can be ascertained during an engagement. I wish you two could only get as far as that. The rest would come." Lady Betty sighed when she thought of a row of rejected suitors.

Mrs. Goddard added her testimony. " Once a man makes love to you you'll have done with ideas, and enquiries, and all that."

The conversation languished, and Sarah took the opportunity of telling Lady Betty that if it was quite convenient they would leave

Woodstock on Monday—in eight days' time. When the friends had left the room, Mrs. Goddard observed that to-day they seemed more hardened in their decision to go away.

"Oh! I don't know, Lucy. You misunderstood them. I have never before felt so near to poor Sally. If they are as serious-minded as appears, they will perhaps leave me comforted."

"They'll leave themselves a pair of old maids," prophesied Mrs. Goddard viciously. "Well, we still have a week, and to-morrow I shall tell Miss Ponsonby my opinion of Miss Butler's character. And take Sir William to talk to her, don't you think?"

"Do. He has been a perfect angel to Sally, who I must own has not given him the consideration she ought. I feel I can do no more."

CHAPTER VI

SECOND FLIGHT

A plain safe intermediate way is cleft
By reason foiling passion : you that rave
Of mad alternatives to right and left
Echo the tempter, madam : and 'tis due
Unto your sex to shun it as the grave,
This later apple offered you.

This apple is not ripe, it is not sweet;
Nor rosy, Sir, nor golden; eye and mouth
Are little moved by it; yet we would eat.
We are somewhat tired of Eden is our plea.
We have thirsted long; this apple suits our drouth;
George Meredith.

In the afternoon of April 25th, Mr. Park, a friend of the Fownes and Butler families, and on this occasion an emissary from Mr. Butler, arrived at Woodstock. He requested an interview with Miss Butler.

" I have come, Miss Butler, to convey to you your father's final decision."

" I am glad of that, as Miss Ponsonby and I are leaving Ireland in six days' time."

" In what Mr. Butler has decided, he does not overlook your ... er ... conduct ... in running away as you did and causing the scandal throughout the country that you have caused—greatly Mr. Butler believes to his detriment. He absolutely disapproves of your determination to leave home. If you carry out your plan you cut yourself off from your parents entirely. In any case you are forbidden to return home at present. I hope you will consider that the rash step you propose may affect your inheritance in later years——"

Mr. Park paused, and coughed nervously.

" This was duly represented to me while I was at Borris."

" There is something more now. Mr. Butler has consented under the above protest to your going to England with Miss Ponsonby, and will make you an annual allowance sufficient for your needs. He is not doing this on his own initiative, but on the advice of those whom he has consulted."

" Ah! it was generous of the Archbishop of Cashel to advise him in that sense."

" Pardon me, Miss Butler, I have not said that Mr. Butler consulted the Archbishop."

" You may take it from me that he did. I shall write and thank the Archbishop. Perhaps—I suspect—I ought to thank you as well."

" I advise you to be careful. The situation is exceedingly delicate."

" I am sure it is. I am not going to wreck it."

" Now—about this money allowance."

" To be sure! What about it ? " Miss Butler's manner was one of perfect polite indifference.

" The amount is six hundred pounds a year."

Miss Butler inclined her head, her face expressionless.

" Are you satisfied ? "

" Naturally I am not satisfied to be cut off from my home. I think that even you, Mr. Park, would agree with me that whatever I have done I have done nothing to merit that! "

" I am speaking of the money."

" Oh, the money! Oh yes! Entirely. I will write my thanks to my father."

Mr. Park was looking at her with a puzzled pained expression.

" You know, Mr. Park:

" ' A son's a son till he gets a wife,
But a daughter's a daughter all the days of her life.' "

" Do you wish me to intercede with your father ? "

" No use at all. It is my mother whom you would have to engage, and with little chance of success. We are better leaving her to the Archbishop."

" I am exceedingly sorry for you."

" Thank you. Would you like to see Lady Betty? "

" I should, and Miss Ponsonby, if I may."

Eleanor went in search of them, and Mr. Park sat reflecting. He had arrived in a severe frame of mind, but really he was not now able to see that this handsome civil young woman had deserved the reprobation that had been her share. After all she had not made any more scandal than her friends had made, with their ill-advised hue and cry after her and her companion. They should have let them go, no harm would have come to them. And now it seemed to him that Miss Butler had forced her father's hand very capably. If Mr. Park had lived in more modern days he would have said that she was now about to get away with it. However he had come here to prevent that if possible, and must do his part faithfully.

He repeated Walter Butler's message to his daughter to Lady Betty and Miss Ponsonby, and then said: " And now it is my duty to say some serious fatherly words to you two ladies."

" Do so—by all means," invited Miss Ponsonby. Mr. Park delivered a weighty address, to which the pair listened with a grave attention which embarrassed him. He detailed the many dreadful mischances, insults, and privations that would be theirs, when they had rendered themselves outcasts, without the support of the Strong Masculine Arm. In no country in the world could women get on alone. Lady Betty marked her approval by emphatic nods.

" Nevertheless thousands do, Mr. Park."

Not ladies of refinement like themselves. Surveying their steady composure, he began to feel that he was wasting his breath.

Looking at Miss Butler he said finally: " I hope I have made clear the consequences of the action which you propose to take."

" Abundantly clear. And we already have them by heart. We are greatly obliged to you. From what we have heard from all our friends, the world is a wicked place. But after all the kindly warnings we have received, I trust we shall not allow it to trample on us."

The interview over, the insurgents stood side by side dignified and gracious and smiled on Mr. Park, thanked him and hoped that if they should be in Ireland again they would have the pleasure of meeting him once more.

Mr. Park remained for two days longer at Woodstock, while Sir William Fownes was engaged in communicating Miss Ponsonby's decision to leave Ireland to her friends, but during the two days neither he nor Mrs. Goddard saw the immovable pair again. On Saturday, May 2nd, having a clear field, Mrs. Goddard arranged to talk to Miss Ponsonby for the last time and also to be present when Sir William Fownes came to say a final word to her. She suggested that Lady Betty should remain away from this interview, which she was glad to do. Lady Betty repeated what she had on another occasion written to Mrs. Goddard. " I sometimes can hardly think the cause is known to anyone but themselves. God knows how it is——"* The many interviews at which she had assisted, had not taken away her confused feeling that the real truth as to why Sally was going away had not transpired. In these days Lady Betty was easily tired, and she was glad to go and sit in the morning-room in which a good light was to be had for her embroidery.

Mrs. Goddard was far from being a malicious woman. She was morally inconsequent to such a degree that she was incapable of bearing a straightforward grudge, or honest resentment against anyone who had hurt or offended her, even if the offence were outrageous. The preposterous young people whom she only desired to help, had, however, not only side-tracked her from her purpose by their absurd questions about being Called to be Saints and so on, but she thought her very poor performance had been due to them, especially to Miss Butler, who had asked such dangerous questions. She therefore projected

* *The Hamwood Papers.*

upon Miss Butler those defects which her conscience was trying to inform her were her own.

She suggested to Miss Ponsonby that they should go to the library at the other end of the hall for a little chat. " It is not, my dear," she said as she sank into an armchair, " that I have anything more to say about your going away."

Miss Ponsonby replied, " That is good . . . we have practically exhausted the subject."

" Not entirely," said Mrs. Goddard, with an air of being judicial, " the question of the kind of friend whom you have chosen, and with whom you are going . . . remains."

" To whom is there a question ? "

" Everyone excepting yourself thinks you have made a very bad choice and that you will never be happy with Miss Butler."

Sarah smiled at the speaker, but made no reply.

" You know her character has been the subject of a great deal of criticism."

" Indeed! And what have Miss Butler's critics to do with me ? "

" You ought to listen to them! "

" I seem to be listening to one—for my sins— at this moment."

" She is a very selfish woman and will entirely dominate you and suck your blood."

No reply.

" She has no principle whatever. I mean moral principle. I dare say her French education is accountable for that. She will do something dreadful, mark my words."

" Can you give me an example of what you mean ? "

" She does not understand virtue, and good living. She only understands conventional appearances. She has a debauched mind. Why, my dear Miss Ponsonby, when she gets you away . . . why . . . she might make love to you."

" I hope she will love me, Mrs. Goddard. She does it so beautifully."

Mrs. Goddard for once in her life looked genuinely shocked, and Miss Ponsonby laughed merrily.

" Why do you laugh ? "

" You are so amusing. You have been here seven days. Out of these, you have spoken to Miss Butler three times and each time you, not she, did all the talking. And now you come to me and talk about a debauched mind. You mustn't. It is an ugly word and offends my young sensibilities. Let us, if you please, consider this conversation closed. I think you must have said more than you meant. The time is past for abusing either of us two; we have practically gone away. But won't you do what I asked you to come here to do ? Comfort Lady Betty, and encourage her to love and think well of us. She isn't well, take care of her. Take care of our good name if you think it is in danger. And take care of yourself—for you are a kind friend—sometimes."

Mrs. Goddard's jaw had dropped open. She shut it with a snap, and said hastily, " I will, my dear."

They sat silent for two or three minutes and then the door opened and Sir William Fownes came in.

" There you are, Sarah! Pray do not move, Mrs. Goddard." He took a chair midway between them. " I hope I do not interrupt your talk. I have come to tell Sarah what her uncle has said to me."

Sarah said nothing, and Sir William continued. " I believe you have not discussed with anyone here what you are going to live on, Sarah."

" It is unnecessary."

" But it is entirely necessary. What if anything happens to Miss Butler ? Well, your relatives are not disposed to do much for you. They never were, but they see they must allow you something. They suggest two hundred pounds a year."

" Thank you. I shall accept it."

" But you can't live on that. You must allow me to increase it."

" Sir William, I am very grateful for all the kindness you have shown me—for your generosity —up to the time when you began to insult me, and I wrote to you on the subject. I would not now touch one penny of yours, if I were starving. Nothing makes me more thankful than the thought that in two days I shall be out of your house."

" Oh, speak to her, Mrs. Goddard! She is altogether mistaken."

" I am not."

" Well . . . I don't know about mistaken, Sir William——"

" You see, Mrs. Goddard has seen everything that in the past few months I have written to you."

" I tell you you have imagined what you call my insults."

" No, I have not. I have objected to your improper speeches to me, to your following me about, seeking occasions for being alone with me, trying to pet me as though you were my lover. I have told you repeatedly that I would not be treated in these ways. You have taken no notice; you have persecuted me. You have taken advantage of the fact that I would not let Lady Betty know. She *would* have known if I had stayed longer, for other people have noticed your attitude and behaviour towards me."

" Sarah, I will swear on the Bible that I never meant——"

" What does your swearing signify, father and grandfather, and false husband——"

" I will never offend you again. I love you too well. It will be terrible if you go away. Stay here and do exactly as you like. I will double your allowance or you shall have as much more as you like. I'll give you more than that miserable two hundred even if you do go away. Lady Betty would indeed wonder if you took nothing from me . . . from us——"

" I won't touch your money. I never want to see or hear of you again. I detest you, and your mean conduct."

" My dear. I implore you on my knees to stay and test me. You shall never complain again. Mrs. Goddard——"

" If the whole world were kneeling at my feet I would not change my resolution. I shall trust myself to an honourable decent friend. I shall live and die with Miss Butler."

" Mrs. Goddard, reason with her! "

" Can't you see it is of no use, Sir William ? "

" *You* don't think I would persecute Sarah, surely ? "

" I must say I think you might. You see, I know men."

" Oh God! Sarah! "

" Please make an end, Sir William. I have had enough. You must understand that I am my own mistress and intend to do as I please. If any attempt is made to use force to prevent me, you will find that I shall make a great deal more trouble than I have done yet. I warn you."

" Well, Sarah, will you promise that if ever you are in real need of money, you will let *me* know first ? Will you ? "

" If you wish to be the person who informs my relations I will. I won't take yours—mind that. That's all I will do. What you have from me is my gratitude for the past—for the future, nothing. Coward! "

The word was like a flung stone and cut like a flint.

She got up and went out of the room, leaving her two hearers speechless. Mrs. Goddard was as one stunned. Sir William strode to and fro like one demented.

Presently Mrs. Goddard said, " For God's sake, Sir William, go and put some cold water over your head—you might burst a blood vessel."

" What shall I do, what shall I do? "

" *Compose* yourself. Keep up appearances. Remember it is true what she says—people are watching you—and think of Betty—here—go in the garden and get the air. I'll stay here until you have got rid of that flush on your face, and then we'll go to them together." She opened the window and pushed Sir William outside.

Practical Mrs. Goddard! It was in such eventualities that she had her wretched uses.

In the morning-room Lady Betty had laid down her needlework. She sat thinking of the interview that was taking place in the library. She knew that Sir William intended to augment generously the scanty annual sum which Sarah's friends had agreed to give her. Sally had been offhand and disobliging to Sir William and she hoped that the gift would excite compunction in the recipient. Poor Sally! She must not go away with nothing, when the undeserving Miss Butler was going away with quite a nice little fortune for a single woman. The frothing scum of sordid experience which made Mrs. Goddard's mind had blown in Lady Betty's direction, and in her tired and confused condition had had its contaminating effect upon her. She was not disposed to share the good opinion of Miss Butler which Mr. Park had expressed. Mr. Park had mentioned Miss Butler's home difficulties as being great and that her treatment had in his opinion been too severe; she must however have been a bad daughter and had certainly been a bad influence on Sally, who had, after all, been a good and loving daughter to herself until she had fallen deeply under that influence. One must of course be charitable, but . . . Here Lady Betty shook her head, and charity had to step into the background.

At this moment the door opened and closed upon Miss Butler herself, who coming to her said, " Would you allow me to take this opportunity of talking to you a little ? "

Lady Betty braced herself. " Oh! Yes . . .

my dear . . . if there is still something to be said. Sit down, will you not."

" Lady Betty, I am older than Sally, and I feel a great responsibility for what I am doing."

Lady Betty replied, " I am glad that you feel it, for then you will know what I and Sir William have felt."

" I want to assure you that for better or worse, for richer or for poorer, in sickness or in health, I shall take care of Sally."

" You must not use the words of our marriage service. It is not suitable."

" I know of no better way of saying what I mean to do. When we are gone away I shall have to comfort the great distress which Sally will feel for a long time. I may perhaps have to be something of the mother to her whom she has missed."

Lady Betty asked stiffly, " Anything else, Miss Butler ? "

" If she ever repents and wishes to return here I shall bring her. And . . . I shall try my utmost with the help of God to be as fit a friend as may be to the lovely and innocent thing that is Sally. We shall never forget that we are ladies of quality, and that our standard is to be the highest we can attain. I can promise that you will hear that of us."

Her pleading voice melted Lady Betty. But she turned and put her hand accusingly on her young companion's shoulder.

" What are you as a daughter, Miss Butler ? "

" I have been all I had a chance to be."

" Your own mother thinks so ? "

" Lady Betty, I never discuss my parents. But for once, for Sally's sake, in strict confidence, I will tell you that my mother is not quite sane about me. That is why the Archbishop of Cashel, who knows about it, advised my people to let me live away—he got them to send me to London. It is by his advice that they are now giving me the means of living away again. But . . . I am not a bad daughter. The Archbishop would tell you I am not. And . . . may God bless *you* . . . for sheltering me here."

" Poor girl! Poor girl! I have been unjust to you. Does Sally know this ? "

" Yes. I do not say much to her, but she has seen it for herself. But I want to tell you that I am not going to be selfish. If Sally wants to be married, I will help her all I can. And I don't want to take her away from you. I want you to write to her, show her you love her, and see her again. When we have a house of our own we want you to be the first to enter it."

" How can you afford a house ? "

" I have always had a liberal allowance, and I have saved some of it for a long time. We shall have enough. We are not going to London but to a tiny cottage which belongs to me—in North Wales."

" Well, Sir William is giving Sally an allowance."

" Forgive me, but I don't think Sally will accept it. You see she wouldn't like both to leave you, and take your money. You can understand that. I hope you won't press her to take it, at any rate now. Of course it is very generous and good of you and Sir William, but please wait until you have visited us. And you will come, won't you ? "

" Miss Butler, I still don't understand why this

has to be. Think of the comments that will arise.
It is not only you two who will suffer, people
will say that I did not take care of Sally or that
because of something that happened when she
was here she *had* to go away." As she said it
Sarah's words came back to Lady Betty. " It
is my duty to go." Duty to go! What! Why . . .

Suddenly Lady Betty clasped her hands and
wrung them together, and turned to Miss Butler
with horrified appeal.

" Miss Butler . . . Eleanor . . . Not *that*——"

In an instant Eleanor, the intuitive, was on her
knees beside Lady Betty with her arms round
her. " No! No! You must not think dreadful
things. A thought can come to anyone. But you
must not let it. Put it away. Put it right away.
You know when we are tired we can have a bad
dream. Don't dream. Think of Sally and me.
Don't you know we count on you and Sir
William to be our friends—our best and truest
friends—for always ? "

Lady Betty, collapsed and sobbing, leant to the
strong young arms. " Oh, my dear, what has
come to me ? Am I so bad . . . so bad ? "

" No indeed! No indeed! We are all tired.
You must pray for us all."

The door opened and Sarah entered. She came
to them quickly, with fear in her face.

" Sally, isn't it true that we·count on Lady
Betty and Sir William to be our best and truest
friends, for always ? "

" Sure it's true," Sarah said. She knelt down
by them and took Lady Betty's hands in hers.
" We couldn't do without it at all. And Sir
William has just told me it's ours."

I

The door opened quietly and Sir William and Mrs. Goddard stepped across the threshold. Then they saw that Lady Betty was in Miss Butler's arms, and Miss Butler was murmuring something to her, and Sally . . . yes Sally, was wiping away her tears.

Mrs. Goddard twitched Sir William's sleeve sharply. They backed silently out of the room and closed the door.

*   *   *   *   *

At the time of sunset on the same day Eleanor and Sarah, from the windows of an upper room, looked out over the fine flower-garden and beautiful wooded estate of Woodstock and beyond it to the distant landscape. Sarah leaned her forehead against the shutter, Eleanor stood silent beside her. They were looking at Ireland.

Sarah said at last, " It is good-bye for ever to all this."

" Yes. I cannot think of anything now that is likely to bring us back to the old country."

" If it is hard for me, and I have no home, what must it be for you ? "

" Oh, perhaps no harder! You know, Sally, women are not supposed to love their country."

" I don't think they *do* care much. I am quite sure that Mr. Speaker Ponsonby cares more for his country than Lady Betty does. But we two *do* care."

" Well . . . God save Ireland! " Eleanor said heavily.

" And us! "

Chapter VII

TO WALES

When in disgrace with fortune and men's eyes
I all alone beweep my outcast state,
And trouble deaf heaven with my bootless cries,
And look upon myself, and curse my fate,
Wishing me like to one more rich in hope,
Featur'd like him, like him with friends possess'd,
Desiring this man's art and that man's scope,
With what I most enjoy contented least;
Yet in these thoughts myself almost despising
Haply I think of thee,—and then my state
Like to the lark at break of day arising
From sullen earth, sings hymns at heaven's gate;
For thy sweet love remember'd such wealth brings
That then I scorn to change my state with kings.
                    Shakespeare. Sonnet XXIX.

On Sunday, May 3rd, the heartsearching talks and exhausting interviews were over, and Sir William spread what oil he could on the troubled waters of his household by reading prayers to them.

All that the two friends could say to one another about their situation was, that if they had not run away as they had done at first, they would have had to do it at the last, but that on the whole having being compelled to face the family clamour, they had not come off badly. To most girls and women of their time, force would have been applied—they would have been saved from themselves regardless of their legal and human rights; but these two, during their thrust for freedom, had made it evident to their friends that in their case force would be worse than useless. They had, therefore, proceeded calmly and openly with their plans, and completed their arrangements unhindered. They had chartered the tiny cabin of a small boat which was leaving Waterford Harbour for Milford Haven with a consignment of butter and bacon, and a chaise was already in the Woodstock yard in readiness to take themselves and their small belongings to Waterford. As an early start was necessary next morning in time to catch the tide, leave-takings took place overnight. Only Lady Betty was not told of the time of their departure, that she might be spared the agitation of a further parting with Sally. Mary Carryl had undertaken to see them go.

Early on May 4th Sarah knocked at Mrs. Goddard's door, and asked to see her. But Mrs. Goddard had received Sarah's embrace on the previous evening, and having taken up her neutral position again upon the fence, could not be dislodged from the other side of her closed door.

After a week upon tenterhooks for fear she should betray someone, or something, she would not encourage the final exit by giving the fugitives a friendly send-off, and declined to emerge from her fastness.

But when Sarah had gone away from her door she opened her window and leaned out. The chaise had not come to the house door, but was standing some distance down the main drive. After an interval she looked out again, and saw

the two friends below taking whispered leave of
Mary Carryl. She saw them laugh and rally the
maid, and shake hands with her, and made a
note that they set out "as merry as possible."*
But when they had turned away she only saw
their backs, and the figure of Mary Carryl left
standing near the steps, crossing herself and
praying for them, was not a merry sight. Mrs.
Goddard drew her head inside the window, and
getting off her fence experienced a very strange
twinge of conscience. She repressed it by
reminding herself that she had still a great deal
to do. She did not usually remember obligations,
but she realized that only two days ago she had
given her word to Sarah that she would defend
her and her companion and would try to silence
the flood of gossip and criticism which was about
to spread over Kilkenny County, and would help
and comfort Lady Betty. She judged that Sir
William was in an unstable state and might fall
into some ditch or other and need to be extricated.
It was plain that she must stay longer at Woodstock, where she was sure of her welcome.

As Sir William and Lady Betty Fownes came
down to breakfast Mary Carryl met them at the
foot of the stairs.

"If you please, my lady, I was to tell you that
the Ladies was obliged to leave at six o'clock,
the way they would catch their boat. They
wouldn't let you be waked early and you very
tired. They sent their love, my lady, and
hoping to see you before long."

"Oh, Carryl! I *am* sorry . . . it *was* kind . . .
were they . . . comfortable ? "

* See Mrs. Goddard's diary, *The Hamwood Papers.*

" I put enough things to eat with them for half a week, my lady."

"Were they . . . did they . . .?" Lady Betty could not finish her question.

" They did so, my lady. The pair of them was in tears of grief—God be good to them! "

" I think He will be, Carryl."

" If your ladyship was to think you could spare me by and by, there's Mary Joseph Dillon would take my place—I'd go and look after the Ladies the way no one would impose on them."

" That's an idea," said Sir William, who was standing by. " If you can spare Carryl, hadn't she better go ? "

" Well . . . she could."

" I thank you, my lady. The Ladies said to me they was going in the country. It isn't wages I'd want, but if they had a cow or chickens or the like I'd make money for them."

" Get the steward to help you to write a letter, and bring it to her ladyship to address," ordered Sir William.

Now that the friends had gone away Mrs. Goddard found her task more easy. Whenever she went abroad in Society, she was cornered privately and asked questions. Her replies were tart. No, the Ladies had not run away, they had gone openly. There was no material for a scandal, no man in it, it was a romantic friendship. They were both of age and could do as they pleased.

Had one of them influenced the other ?

With a vivid recollection of the younger lady's forceful interview with Sir William, Mrs. Goddard thought not—one was as strong-minded and

wilful as the other. When it was suggested to
her that presently there would be a Prodigal's
Return, she thought not—they would carry out
their intentions. On this point conviction had
come even to sceptical Mrs. Goddard, for she
had heard Sarah's " I will live and die with
Miss Butler."

Mrs. Hamerton, the emissary who had taken
Miss Butler to the shelter of her sister's house,
was a friend of the Butler family. Her daughter
in an excited letter to Mrs. Goddard circulated
details of the flight, which Mrs. Goddard may or
may not have believed—she was a shrewd dis-
counter of her friends' exaggerations. According
to the letter the fugitives had been " stopped by
an underservant of Sir W. F. in a Carr in Men's
Clouths." " 'Tis really wonderful from the
accounts we hear of their expedition that either
of them is alive."* The writer had just dined at
Kilkenny Castle and went on to relate, " Miss B.
left the Castle just as the family went in to dinner
and was not missed for two hours. 'Tis supposed
that she changed her clouths in the Porch and
got on a Horse (which she had never done before)
to ride several miles of a dark night. The Family
. . . imagined she was gone to marry some Body
but did not know who to fix on."

Mrs. Goddard was for the moment an effective
help in checking rumours round about Kilkenny
and the neighbouring counties, but nothing in
the end could prevent the embellishment of the
story with imaginary details purporting to be
facts. The fugitives had jumped out of windows,
climbed walls, one broke a leg, one escaped in

* See *The Hamwood Papers*.

the clothing of a groom, they had carried pistols, they had crossed mountains in the dark. These and other reports excited public curiosity about the intrepid ladies as much as they annoyed and pained their relatives. The real fact however was that they had arranged their exit from Ireland well, had departed quietly, reached Waterford successfully, and but for Sarah's unfortunate illness would have got away in peace and have been able to treat with their friends from a distance. All the noise had been made by those who had suspected that there were " gentlemen concerned " and had hunted them.

Soon Mrs. Goddard went where she might glean information. At the house of friends of Miss Butler she heard that Sir William's attentions to Miss Ponsonby were being whispered about. She warned Sir William to be very careful in what he said about Miss Butler, and to make the most of the fact of her share in the romance. She called at the Castle where nothing was said to her. Later, when she received an invitation to the Castle, she would not go. She provided a thrill for Lady Betty and two friends by visiting and describing to them the barn in which the two runaways had spent the night. When all aristo-cratic Ireland began to hum with the story of the flight, and to express sympathy with the families of the fugitives, she lay low and said as little as possible. On the whole Mrs. Goddard achieved a noteworthy negative position with regard to the affair. She forgot that Miss Butler had a " debauched mind " and defended her by maintaining the romantic friendship theory, which ruled out any involvement with male persons. Whatever, in the eighteenth century, a romantic friendship was supposed to imply, that she helped their relations to uphold. And since no terrible scientific names were in existence to describe phenomena of the kind, the escapade remained romantic, to the entire peace of the subjects themselves.

Nevertheless, romantic friendships pursued in this extreme manner—friends, prospects, luxury, and above all, social position being thrown to the winds—had no parallel within the experience of high Society. It was true that occasionally a lady of quality had been known to elope with some groom, highwayman or beguiling foreigner, to repent later at ignominious leisure. There were even a few cases recorded in which the lady never had repented, and had disappeared into a contented oblivion, but the flight of these two young and beautiful women together called for some separate explanation. There were Irish men who had known the brilliant and sweet-natured Miss Butler both at home and in London, and could testify to the competition for her society that had obtained wherever she had been ; there were others who could not forget the charming elfish Miss Ponsonby and her enchanting dance at the Dublin ball. Lastly, there were family friends who, on reviewing the homes from which the two ladies had gone away, were left wondering—although women must of course submit to whatever home conditions fate provided for them—whether there might not have been something peculiarly intolerable to these sensitive high-spirited women in one —or both—of their homes which could furnish some shadow of excuse for them.

Mrs. Goddard could say with truth that she knew next to nothing of Miss Butler's history and home conditions, but she was known as a friend of the Fownes, and when questioned about Miss Ponsonby was obliged to retreat from the dangerous quicksands of indirect reply to direct interrogation. Whispers began to circulate more freely. Rumours about Sir William's " gallantry " reached Sir William's daughter, Mrs. Tighe, who preferred never to believe them. But in view of the existence of rumours which were bound to spread, and in the interests of all the parties concerned, Mrs. Goddard began to contemplate retreat to Dublin, or even to England, as soon as might be possible.

That the fugitives, having carried their day with callous boldness, should have gone away in deep depression probably entered no one's mind, certainly not Mrs. Goddard's. Lady Betty felt somewhat consoled on hearing that they had gone away in " tears of grief " that had provoked the solicitude of her servant, Carryl. Sarah, homeless and affectionate and grateful, was torn by her conflicting feelings and choice, and wept as they drove away, while Eleanor, parting with the home in which she was rooted by blood, and by centuries of family tradition, being, moreover, under the inexorable ban of her parents, went with a sword in her heart which could not be plucked out, but had to be endured. These two had in the country of their birth a comparatively small horizon, which they had outgrown; nevertheless Ireland was their mother as no other country could or would ever be, and their love was rooted in her tempestuous heart. On that fourth of May they left their country never again to return. The early morning sun streaming in upon them, as their conveyance passed along the lonely Irish road, found them clinging together and sobbing bitterly under this cruel tearing up of roots. The rotund grey-haired captain of their boat received the great ladies from Woodstock politely, cap in hand. He called two of his hands to take their things to the little cabin, which had been scrubbed out, and only smelt moderately of tobacco, stale spirits, pitched ropes and fried herrings. Out of several folded tarpaulins and sails he made a bed for them on the cabin floor. He said they would have fine weather, and with a sufficient wind should arrive at their destination the next morning. And he showed them where they could sit on the little deck without getting in the way of the navigation of the boat if they chose to take the air by day. He said he would take as much care of them as if they were diamonds, and they were to ask him for anything they needed. He retreated to a minute glory-hole over the little hold, and apparently slept through the day there, as they saw no more of him until next morning. The boat reached the open sea, and they spent some hours on deck while the coast of Ireland remained in sight. They were both silent for a long time. When land had disappeared Eleanor took Sarah's hand and said softly, " Dear heart, would you go back ? " and Sarah, lifting a passionate face, said, " I'd rather drown in these waters, God knows. *You* are my Ireland."

" I think we shall not have to carry Ireland as a snail carries its shell on its back. All that it has been to us we shall have."

" As an ingredient of our life blood."

" Yes, just that. But from now onwards we must do the growing which our people would not allow us . . . new life——"

" How long it seems since we sat in your room and talked of *noblesse oblige*."

" And I, then, with this day in my heart! "

" How long the time was until I was twenty-one. Ages and ages. I must have been a stupid companion to Lady Betty."

" And now we have to live all that we have waited for. This wind is getting chilly; let us remember your throat. Will you not come into the cabin? You are still so pale. Come here to me."

Under the warmth of Eleanor's cloak Sarah closed her eyes and slept. A pleasant night followed, with little wind and a moonlit sea. They had what sleep they could get on their hard bed, the boat rocking, the gear creaking, the water slapping the sides of the boat, and a watching man tramping on the deck. Once they woke to fresh sounds. The tramping man had turned in. Dawn was coming up, and the man at the tiller was singing in a clear young voice. He sang about somebody's ball, and then about a blue-eyed Queen of his Heart ; finally, he sang a crooning Litany of Mary, Star of the Sea. The friends listened with pleasure. His singing had not disturbed his companions, but when the louder strains ceased the softer refrain of the Litany roused the Captain. A hoarse growl came from his shelter. " Howld yer noise, ye blasted Son of Satan—wud ye wake the Ladies ? "

Silence, and then murmured apologies from the

By permission of Mrs. Whittington Herbert of Llangollen

LADY IN A TALL HAT
(Said to be a portrait of Sarah Ponsonby)

singer, who, having followed his habitual salutation of the coming day, had clane forgot himself.
About six o'clock in full daylight the Captain
appeared at the cabin door, and the Ladies sat
up to receive him. He carried a can of hot beer,
and in a hairy paw two slices of dry bread. He
offered the ladies this breakfast which they
accepted with smiles and gracious words. They
told him they had enjoyed the singing, and the
Captain praised God that it had been fit for
ladies to hear, and later, on relieving the singer
at the tiller, comforted him with the same
reflection and caused him to pass the open cabin
door with a rich blush added to his clear red
complexion.

In two hours more the travellers landed in their
new country.

After arriving at Milford Haven the friends
travelled to Birmingham that they might outfit
themselves incognito for their new life. They
caused the frocks in which they had graced the
Dublin ball and some other fine clothing to be
sold. No more of such festivities would be theirs.
Somehow they knew they had grown too old for
these, and of course they were going to need
country clothes. In their own day the nearest
thing to modern sports-clothing was a lady's
travelling outfit, the plain dress called a habit
and a beaver hat. In this dress ladies of quality
took their long journeys by coach or post-
chaise. The dress was useful for riding if necessary, but it had more frequently the˙ wider use.
The habits were worn in fine colours such as blue,
green, or scarlet, under dark comfortable travel-
ling-cloaks. Neither a Butler nor a Ponsonby

proposed to make an impression of lowliness or humility in their new sphere. *Noblesse oblige* was to extend to personal appearance, and what they wore was to be worthy of their status.

They sought out a first-class tailor and had their habits made in a deep blue, with lighter-weight duplicates in fine black cloth. They had their thick fair hair cut conveniently short, and ordered, as the very newest head-gear, the silk hats which had just appeared in London. They were careful as to accessories, and bought smart gloves with gauntlets and cravats of the finest Indian muslin. This type of clothing was worn after their own days and far into Victorian times, although after railways came into existence it was chiefly worn by riders. In any case, just as a Butler and a Ponsonby had set the fashions at the Dublin ball, so they preposed to set them now on the London to Ireland highroad. And very smart and distinguished they appeared in the new outfit.

No runaways, no fugitives are going to be seen in the Valley of Llangollen, good people! But first and last, ladies of standing. Free. And Ourselves.

In the eighteenth century the Valley of Llangollen was a quiet spot and the village itself very small. It contained the old posting houses, the Hand and the Lyon Inns, and large numbers of travellers to and from Ireland used the inns. The district was very beautiful. The sides of the mountains were covered with sheep farms, and sprinkled with fir and larch woods, and at the bottom of the valley the beautiful river Dee took its impetuous course seawards. The village was within driving distance of Shrewsbury,

By permission of the County Studios, Monmouth

RUIN OF VALE CRUCIS

Oswestry, Chester, Ruthin, and other towns, and about the countryside were the seats of well-known families. But the population was sparse and, as in Ireland, highwaymen and other robbers were not unknown. The people were not uncivilized; they were kindly, friendly, musical, religious, superstitious. They had the same beliefs in ghosts and spirits, and the evil eyes of witches, that obtain among most of us to-day. Living was exceedingly cheap, and the poor were not so poor as to make a grievance of it. They were on the whole well clothed and fed. If they were not, the spirits that dwelt in whisky bottles and kegs knew why not. The ancient Castle of Dinas Bran, high on its hilltop over-hanging the village, was haunted by the ghosts of past days, and the ruined Cistercian Abbey of Vale Crucis which lay on its north-western border was crowded with them. There were similar ruins of similar churches and monasteries in Kilkenny, compensated, as in Llangollen, for the destroying hand of the Protestant style, by the existence of ghosts. For anything that we know to the contrary, there were people walking about in the Valley of Llangollen, and equally in Kilkenny, who were destined in the future to walk there as disembodied spirits. There were certainly two, who had chosen Llangollen for their dwelling-place, who would live on there when their bodies were gone from the place. But the people did not know that.

Meantime, the village perceived walking about in the flesh two very interesting strangers. Their main peculiarity was that, being young and handsome, they should have chosen this valley to dwell in, while their only claim to be considered uncanny was that they had no fear of ghosts, but had actually bought the little haunted house on the hillside, and were just about to rebuild it. So, while the Irish aristocracy were enjoying the scandalous tale of their friendship, and exaggerating to an unbelievable extent the details of an absurdly conceived flight, the simple people of Llangollen were getting their thrills from direct contacts with the newcomers. For they were gracious, courteous, kindly to everybody, from the opulent owners of the inns, to the humblest labourers on farms or limekilns. The owner of the post-office, with whom they lodged, had no need to whisper that they belonged to great people, whenever you looked at or spoke to them, you felt their Quality.

Meanwhile, in Ireland the remainder of the month of May was not a happy time at Woodstock. Mrs. Goddard occupied herself as has been recorded. Lady Betty became more drooping and frail, and was glad to get letters from Llangollen from the travellers thanking and cheering her, and telling her of their comfortable little lodging, and of the business they were at in preparing the little house on the hillside for occupation. Lady Betty's daughter, Mrs. Tighe, came to stay with her. Sir William had become very difficult and cross-tempered, impossible to please—seemed to dislike everyone who came near him. The loss of the presence of Sarah Ponsonby was a dire calamity and he was suffering acutely, for the phantasies which for many months past he had indulged had now deserted him, leaving him in deep torments with which he could not cope. He had a severe attack of illness, and on June 6th told Mrs. Goddard in the presence of his daughter that his illness was a punishment for a state of mind which was his own fault. A few days later he died, and the news of his death was sent to Miss Ponsonby.

A tender and loving letter came to Lady Betty from Sarah, expressing the sympathy and sorrow of both friends.

" What will she do, Sally ? " Eleanor asked.

" I think she was forgetting to love him," Sarah replied. " He was so often rude and unkind to her. If she can recover her own health she may do vastly better without him . . . now. How I wish I had never gone to Woodstock."

After Sir William's death, Mrs. Goddard, believing her task to be complete, left Woodstock and went her sordid way, visiting her friends and amusing herself in her usual flighty irresponsible manner. But Lady Betty did not recover. She drooped farther, and one evening in July she quietly let go her life, and in less than a month after Sir William's death was laid by his side.

And Sarah who had loved her was shocked, and grieved exceedingly, although in Ireland people were always dying. She asked Eleanor, " Do you think she knew ? "

And Eleanor said, " I . . . don't . . . know . . . Sally. But I think, in the end, she did. We may thank God that she had no blame for you. And now they are both where there may be a new chance of understanding."

Sarah recalled the talks of Lady Betty and Mrs. Goddard about marriage, which had once hurt her so much.

K

" Yes . . . perhaps they are remembering now, that they once loved one another."

The cottage on the hillside began to grow and expand. But before the building had got far something happened to the Ladies. Someone was dead. They looked very sad, they wore black clothing, they walked about arm in arm looking at the ground. Only they looked up with illuminating smiles if anyone who passed them shyly called upon them the blessing of God. Later in July a smart middle-aged Irish woman arrived in the village—no. other than Mary Carryl. And she told the valley that great ladies were about to live in the new cottage, Plas Newydd, ladies who had been used to twenty servants; and she magnified her own office, as their housekeeper, accordingly.

PART II

I MEET THE LADIES

            1785
Sept. 24th. From 7 till 9, in sweet converse with
            the delight of my heart.
Oct.   7th. A day of strict retirement, sentiment
            and delight.
Nov. 21st. A day of peace and delight.
Dec.   7th. My Sweet Love! A silent pensive day.
Dec. 12th. A day of the most perfect and sweet
            retirement.
            1788
Jan.   8th. A day of sweet and silent retirement.
Jan. 31st. A day of sweet and delicious retire-
            ment.
Feb. 24th. A day of most delicious and exquisite
            retirement.
Mar. 18th. A day of sweetly enjoyed retirement.
            1789
Jan. 21st. A day of delicious retirement.
May   7th. A day of sweet occupation and en-
            joyed retirement.
Sept. 24th. A day of sweet retirement.
Dec.   7th. A day of such sweet retirement.
Dec. 18th. A day of delicious retirement.
            1791
Feb.   2nd. A day of sweet retirement.
Mar.   9th. A day of silent and sweet retirement.
            JOURNAL OF E.B. AND S.P.
            Written by E.B.

Chapter VIII

PLAS NEWYDD

Ah, but that's the world's side, there's the wonder,
There they see you, praise you, think they know you!
There in turn I stand with them and praise you—
Out of my own self I dare to phrase it.
But the best is when I glide out from them,
Cross a step or two of dubious twilight,
Come out on the other side—the novel
Silent silver lights and darks undreamed of
Where I hush and bless myself with Silence.

Robert Browning.

THE little house, Plas Newydd, did not take long
to rebuild, nor cost much money. The items that
make our modern houses costly to build and
expensive to maintain, were in 1778 unknown,
and were not missed. There were no closed
ranges, cold- and hot-water systems, fixed baths,
nor drainage systems. There was no gas, nor
electric light. Royalty itself had only candles or
oil lamps to light its darkness. Of course, at that
time domestic work was harder, and the affairs
of the toilet when thoroughly carried out took
longer; but that was all. Plas Newydd had cold
water, and coal was cheap. To the friends,
accustomed to life in large imperfectly warmed
houses, Plas Newydd promised to be very
comfortable. Upstairs they had a bedroom,

and a dressing-room, and a guest or " state " bedroom. Below they had a library, an "eating-parlour " and a third room. All these rooms had fireplaces, for this plateau on the mountain side could be cold in winter. The kitchen and maids' rooms completed the little establishment.

The two friends were strong healthy women, and the luxury which they had previously known had meant as little as possible to either. The great manor house of Woodstock could never have been to Sarah Ponsonby more than a charitable roof spread over a poor young kinswoman by kindly relatives who had taken some of her life-blood in exchange. The Castle of Kilkenny was only a wife's home until her widowhood, when she had to transfer herself to a dower-house, and make room for the successor to the title or estates and his family. Great houses never reckoned to be a home for unmarried daughters. Of course this same arrangement persists in the twentieth century, although the enormous number of well-to-do unmarried women with incomes that are really their own, and who can now make what they please of their own lives, had no parallel in the eighteenth century.

To the two exiles, still suffering from the fatigue and depression of their unhappy years, the creation of Plas Newydd, this home of their own—which was bringing with it, as it grew, the realization of their passion for personal freedom—brought intoxicating pleasure. They knew however that they must canalize their feelings and organize their activities, and that everything in

PLAS NEWYDD

this new life must be in suitable proportion to everything else.

They would have to wait at least three or four months before the house was ready for occupation, and they had fine summer weather before them. Both felt that what they needed was a retreat into the wilderness. And so, day after day for many weeks, they climbed the mountains and explored hills and valleys, sat by rushing streams or in bracken and heather or sometimes among stones, and absorbed the beauty of this place of their choice. A great deal of simple pagan affection and worship was given to Mother Earth and she replied by nourishing the rootlets which they at once began to put down in the country of their adoption. On the hilltops pain began to abate, they became able to talk calmly of all that they had left behind them, and repressions were smoothed out. It was long since they had walked together by the river under the walls of Kilkenny Castle, or in the beautiful woods of Woodstock—of late they had either been parted or in such hurried and anxious circumstances that they could not talk of anything but the immediate future. They had both been so tired, and Sarah fairly recently so sick. Now unlimited time was their own, and the present really belonged to them. But now they did not only talk, they were often silent half the day, or they simply curled up and slept, sometimes in the sun, sometimes in corners sheltered from wind among the crags. They ate with increasing enjoyment the *al fresco* meals they carried with them, and soon they grew bright-eyed and began to laugh, became burnt to a

healthy colour by wind and sun, and fresh energy
returned to them.

" The hills have been good to us," said Eleanor
at last. " But now for life below." And Sarah
smiled a slow dreaming smile and said, " By all
means—if it is really there. I suppose to prove
that we had better go to Oswestry and buy
chairs."

Buying simple necessary things, their innate
good taste enabled them to make their little house
beautiful. With so few natural or architectural
advantages it might have looked dull and poor.
But these two, with their appreciation of form and
colour, brought in unerringly what was suitable,
and the place achieved a style of its own which
quickly attracted attention. Finely chosen objects
needed a fine background, and no background
that was within their reach could be as effective
as one of old oak. Old oak at that time was
neither dear nor hard to come by. And close at
hand was the ancient Abbey of Vale Crucis,
which for two or three centuries had been
allowed to crumble away. Some of its carved
roofing and stained glass had been absorbed in
two local churches, but a quantity of debris
remained—the substance of papistical toys for
which Methodist Wales had no regard nor use.
The friends were able to secure the unwanted
fragments, and under Sarah's skilful planning
oak panels lined the walls and slender pillars and
Gothic arches enclosed or outlined windows,
alcoves or doors in the rooms. The little carved
saints, angels or devils that had once made of the
Abbey Church a living expression of religious
phantasy and creative endeavour, and that now

CARVED DOOR, PLAS NEWYDD

in mouldering heaps lay in the dust, were lifted up, and renewed existence on doors, walls or in shaded corners of Plas Newydd. When these little ghosts of former days had ranged themselves in the shadows, they gave dignity and confidence to the house, as well as a strangely mystical impression to those who came into it from without.

Immediately behind the house there was a deep ravine filled with trees and having in its centre a rushing stream. About half-way down the dip by the path on the right of the stream a spring issued from the bank. Considering what they could do with a beautiful old font and some other stones collected from Vale Crucis Abbey the friends decided to make a drinking-fountain in this place. Sarah's feeling of artistic fitness and the feelings that had come of Eleanor Butler's Catholic education, would not allow them to lose the fine old stone receptacle, or put it to mere domestic uses; it was given back to Nature with dignity and reverence, enclosed in a Gothic arch, and built securely into the bank. Stone seats on either side provided for rest and meditation, and the little erection was not the less the beginning of a church because it was now chiefly at the disposal of elves, water nixies or woodland creatures and dripping with water and covered with moss. Built in on either side were two large blocks of stone on which were cut simple verses in words of one and two syllables which told its history to the inhabitants of Protestant Llangollen who passed that way, and reminded them of their ancestors' treatment of the noble church to which it had belonged.

Drink gentle pilgrim from the Well
Thus sacred, in this hollow dell.
Drink deep! Yet ere thy yearning lip
Touches the draught it longs to sip
Pray for the souls of those who gave
This font that holds the limpid wave.
This holy font which lay o'erthrown
Mid Vale Crucis' shadows brown.
And which the hands of holy men
Have blest, but ne'er can bless again.
Drink happy pilgrim, drink and pray
At morning dawn and twilight grey
Pray for the souls of those who gave
This font that holds the limpid wave.
E.B.   1782.   S.P.

The linking-up of the new home with what was
old was as sound an instinct as had been the
passing of long days facing sky and mountain
tops. The one gave them a comforting sense of
continuity with the past, just as the other lifted
them out of it.

As is the case with all good things, the home
developed slowly. The furnishing included the
buying of books to be read during the approaching winter. To both friends books were a necessity.
Both had come from houses with fine old libra-
ries in which they had been solitary readers.
The rudiments of a sound culture were already
theirs. In their first winter they read voraciously.
Sarah was able, at last, to draw and paint in the
mornings to her heart's content, and relieved her
pent-up spirit by executing formal or decorative
designs, or delicate arabesques or maps of the
world. Eleanor was never tired of reading aloud,
and could do so for several hours on end. For
many hours on many winter days, and in the

succeeding years, the little Abbey ghosts, standing aloof and attentive on the walls, listened with their native composure to the reading of the works of Rousseau or Voltaire or other liberal or philosophic writers, as well as other classics and history in four languages. As time went on and the season permitted it they rented more land, and made a small farm, and a flower- and vegetable-garden. They were soon employing several servants in and out of doors, and among domestic industries carried on at Plas Newydd butter was made, beer was brewed, and the flax for table-linen was spun.

By the time they settled in their new house they were known throughout the district as " the Ladies." The words so entirely expressed them that no one ever thought of calling them anything else. Many fine families lived in the neighbourhood, but only two individuals became in 1778, and remain in 1935, " the Ladies." They established human relations with ease, for they found no one uninteresting, and they had no idea of living under a cloud, or as twin hermits. But they stayed with their caste. They were visited by, and visited neighbours of their own class in a wide district. They selected their friends carefully. They politely withdrew from vulgar or scheming people who sought them by false excuses for their own ends, and by no means admitted to their acquaintance all who wished it. Persons who were pretentious, patronizing, or bad-mannered, seldom entered Plas Newydd once, never twice. In a temple of *noblesse oblige* bad manners were a great sin. The Ladies were good employers, who knew and appreciated good work, but those who worked for them learnt that they were not to be trifled with. They got to know their poorer neighbours on the hillsides, were told their stories, felt for their sorrows, helped their misfortunes, and admired their independence and grit and decency. Nothing was more sincere and open than their own manner to all others, and nothing more remote from their attitude than pose of any kind. Miss Butler's impetuous frank speech sometimes took away the breath of slower people, but they liked its genuineness. They appeared to their world to be entirely different from one another, for happiness made Eleanor expansive and sympathetic, while it made the more passionate Sarah grave and silent, and too full of intense feeling to allow it to run over the surface of things. But all their world knew that nothing else whatever was to the Ladies what they were to one another, and it respected and trusted them because of their deep mutual affection.

The first four years during the creation of Plas Newydd passed quickly and quietly. Communications with Ireland were few. Mr. Chambre of Oswestry conducted their financial business with their relatives. Then in 1782 Mrs. Goddard on her way from Bath to Dublin came to Llangollen, and on their invitation spent a fortnight "with my fair friends in their very pleasant habitation." And very fair they looked, extraordinarily young and good-looking, and happy as she had never seen them before. Mrs. Goddard was not especially susceptible to atmosphere in an ordinary way, she was more susceptible to mutton chops and appearances of wealth. On her first evening at Plas Newydd, the quiet beauty of the little house almost bewildered her. She had expected a small poor place of discipline and retribution, and to hear of all the trials of two young women who knew nothing about housekeeping. And here, instead, was the very pleasant and distinctly well-ordered habitation. But, especially, Mrs. Goddard could not take her eyes away from Miss Ponsonby in her new surroundings, and Miss Butler watched her puzzled face with quiet amusement. This Miss Ponsonby was not the suffering girl who had once entreated her to come to her help, nor the indignant girl whose flung epithet, " Coward," had struck not only Sir William, but had seemed to include herself, and had frightened her. Here was a poised matured woman who had no more need of help from Mrs. Goddard nor from anyone else.

After supper Miss Ponsonby came and stood for a few minutes at the side of the fireplace, and Mrs. Goddard seated before the fire looked up at her and said to herself that it was curious how tall a low ceiling could make you look. Miss Ponsonby at the moment was making a beautiful picture with her dress of dark purple cloth glowing in the firelight and melting into the oak wall behind her. And then that mop of short fair hair powdered with a silvery powder, and the soft creamy cravat! Fascinated, Mrs. Goddard noted the details for transmission to Bath and to Ireland. She glanced smiling at Miss Butler whose tranquil eyes were upon her friend opposite.

" Sarah looks splendid," said the visitor.

" She's very pretty, isn't she ? "

" I'm afraid I never was much good to you, Sarah."

" Oh! but you were, Mrs. Goddard. You said the right things to Sir William. But we have forgotten all the bad old times here."

In the four years since they had met, Miss Butler's supposed bad influence had dropped out of all their memories. The witch in Mrs. Goddard was being exorcized by the spirit which gave its colour to Plas Newydd. As Miss Butler's guest she not only learnt a great deal, but in her subsequent diary could say exceedingly little about it. There was some powerful influence in this place, whether it was religious or whether it was only uncanny, was all one to Mrs. Goddard; it might be either, she did not distinguish. But she was afraid of it. It recalled to her, day after day, that mysterious breeze at the Dublin ball which no one had ever been able to explain to her.

Mrs. Goddard moved in the best circles but she had not before known anything like the unfailing courtesy and consideration that reigned here, towards herself, between the Ladies, and between themselves and their servants. Five years ago, when they were all at Woodstock, she and Lady Betty had remarked on the politeness of Miss Butler and Sarah towards one another. " Exaggerated, don't you think ? " Lady Betty had said. " Oh! *affected*, my dear, and no more likely to last than the usual endearments between lovers. To see much of it would make one tired."

At last Mrs. Goddard went her way, retracing her flighty steps to Bath. In the year after her visit Eleanor Butler's father died, and readjustments as to provision for his daughter had to be made. Mrs. Goddard being again in Dublin was asked about the Ladies' circumstances, but she wrote in reply that she would answer no questions about Miss Butler or Miss Ponsonby. It is unlikely that the Ladies heard of this, but it appears that the little Saints in charge of Plas Newydd had obtained some grace for her.

The year 1785 was a year of anxiety for the Ladies. Eleanor Butler's brother John had been married sixteen years previously, and in his marriage settlement provision had been made for herself, which had now to take effect. Delay was inevitable, and there was also in Ireland great commercial stagnation and financial distress of every kind and the incomes of many rich families were embarrassed or crumbling away. It was inconvenient for the Ladies of Plas Newydd to receive money which was theirs in small irregular sums, under the signatures of various friends, and painful to be unable promptly to discharge their bills as *noblesse oblige* required. There existed no desire on the part of their relatives to keep them short of what was their due, and it was not long before Mr. Chambre had their affairs in order again.

Following changes in the Butler family circle made by Mr. Butler's death, changed conditions began to affect the Ladies. So far they had not had much communication with their Irish friends. No doubt many of those of their own generation, whose last memory of them included the vivid picture of the Dublin ball, had been afraid of making trouble for themselves or for the Ladies

L

by seeking them out. But the story of their happy and successful life had spread to Ireland and a great many people began to correspond with and visit them. It does not appear that Eleanor Butler's sister or brother visited her, but her sister-in-law Lady Anne Butler came twice, and also her little daughter and later all her sons. Sir William Barker, Sarah Ponsonby's good friend came. In the end friends turned up in Llangollen in such large numbers that they found it necessary to keep a journal, in order to remember them, while to keep a record of all the people who came later became impossible. But the visitors found that the Ladies had put ineradicable roots down into their Welsh soil, and were not to be enticed back to the country which they had left under such painful circumstances.

The Ladies did not, however, only entertain their friends at home. They were entertained over a wide area. Their neighbours with large country houses gave breakfasts, luncheons, afternoon parties, supper parties, and at these they spent long days. Often there were good music and singing, or recitations and plays, for the amusement of the guests. The Ladies' presence was always desired at their neighbours' social functions, at which their animation, high spirits and interesting conversation were a large asset in the affair. When Eleanor Butler and Mrs. Crewe, or some other bright spirit, could be got together, the success of a party was assured. As a card-player Miss Ponsonby had great gifts. The men enjoyed their society at all times. "That they should prefer one another to *us*," said a gallant gentleman after one such occasion, " does not surprise me, since they have each drawn a prize in life's lottery, but why *we* have allowed it, I shall never understand. I am persuaded that there is something very much amiss in us men."

If the Ladies, in leaving Ireland, had sought a narrower life, if the retirement in which they continued to rejoice had been a retirement into a soft and idle existence, if they had made in the valley of Llangollen the fewest possible human relationships, and if ideas had been nothing to them, then, notwithstanding their sufficient means of livelihood, they might have continued to exist as scores of well-to-do and presumably educated people do exist in the country, in emptiness and isolation. Long before they had lived for ten years together their minds and spirits might have shrunk, and they might both have deteriorated as companions and friends. And then one might have devoured the other. But while they were young, both had decided, as a result of what they had seen, that friendship, equally with all other relationships, could not live on nothing, but needed careful cultivation. The journal which they kept, and which Eleanor Butler wrote up for three-and-a-quarter years, and afterwards at intervals, affords evidence, (apart from the testimony of their friends) of their steady development, of their ever-growing maturity of mind and outlook, of their health and happiness. It shows too that they lived with a full sense of responsibility, and that they recorded their life, as they lived it, with transparent honesty.

The Journal of E. B. and S. P., written by E. B.

and labelled the " short and simple annals of the poor," was begun in 1785 when the friends had lived together for seven years. It is inimitable in what it conveys of their two lives, and is to so great an extent a love-song, since all the pleasures and happiness it records depend upon their intimate life together, that it is neither to be taken too literally nor to be interpreted nor paraphrased by the mere teller of tales, but only by the poets. The journal is of " We," and when the pen overflows to the " I " of the scribe, it is because some very personal feeling must be given expression.

" How can I acknowledge the kindness and tenderness of my beloved Sally."

Eleanor, who knew most about gardening, looked after the garden, while Sarah, the first object of adoration of Mary Carryl, who had served her for some years before they left their own country, was housekeeper and accountant. But they were seldom far apart. " My Beloved and I went "—as the journal recorded over and over again—" together—everywhere." Sarah was Eleanor's first and last thought. The Beloved had new shoes, drew, or made beautiful things for the home, suffered from toothache, turned a drunken man out of the kitchen—of such little things did the Journalist write. Sally never failed Eleanor— she was a most practical and able friend. For instance, when Eleanor suffered on one occasion from a severe headache: " My beloved made me take an emetic and by that kindness anxiety and tenderness which constitutes the happiness of my life softened the pain which I endured."*

* A harsh domestic remedy for many ills which was popular in those hardy times.

Because of the frequent invasions of visitors they often had insufficient time for directing the affairs of their establishment, but when a quiet day came, and they had it to themselves, the journal proclaimed the special circumstance with expressions of delight. Such days were " most perfect," " delicious and exquisite," " silent and sweet." These days of " sweet retirement " were usually spent in writing, or in study, or in reading to one another. At the end of fifteen years of this life Eleanor was still in the journal singing the canticles of their shared and satisfied days.

" My Sally, my tender my sweet love——"

" How can I acknowledge——"

Very few people who love one another tell one another about it often enough—some forget to perform this simple duty for years. These two never forgot, and yet the task never lost its freshness. Like other mercies of the Lord it was new every morning.

Chapter IX

ELEANOR'S JOURNAL

When, if I think but deep enough
You are wont to answer prompt as rhyme,
And you too, find without rebuff
Response your soul seeks many a time
Piercing its fine flesh stuff.

Robert Browning.

ELEANOR BUTLER'S acute literary sense, and taste for fine writing, never betrayed the journal into anything artificial or cheap. Her record was not one of those unfortunate documents excused as being material for autobiography, which are so often written with one eye on an admiring or interested reading public, but which are invariably only boring. It was not written in order that " We," after being gathered and stored by the reaper, might get some of their own back. This journal speaks of no personal sorrows, rails at no injustice, betrays no one, sounds no religious depths, goes to no extremes of opinion, makes no claim to learning. It is as amazing under its cloud of reserve as in what its lightning shafts—often only by a word or two—reveal. It is never carping, nor sour, nor malicious, although it is not afraid to express likes and dislikes, loves or hatreds ; but sound sentiment and an instinct for goodness colour it throughout. The Ladies themselves used it as a reference to the things in previous years that had needed recording. In a well-spent country life, time runs away so fast, the seasons come and go with such rapidity, that a record of those small events which are not small to those who experience them, is often a necessity, as much a necessity as is to most of us a bank pass-book, a household account book, or a calendar of days and months. It was thus at Plas Newydd.

We read with pleasure the journalist's record of her first and last look at the day or night, for Eleanor's world was always well seen and the sight finely expressed. We can scent the sweet-briar, violets and cherry-trees, and hear the song of the birds in spring. We can see the sun set in flames of crimson and gold. We can enjoy with herself and the Beloved their moonlight walks, we can lean with them over the gate of their field listening in the profound silence of the valley to Thomas Jones playing a sweet pipe on the church-yard wall that hangs over the river. On one night the moon casts her silver light on the mountains where burning heather is flaming. On another night the fiercely burning lime kilns look like glow-worms in the mountains. In October the colours of the beautiful valley entrance her—azure, lilac, silver, green, scarlet, gold. Again in spring she notes down the honey-suckle, wild roses, elder, strawberries, campanula in hedges and banks, and she records elsewhere an evening when the sky is like a sea of blood. These things are not merely seen and recorded, they are recorded because they are felt and lived in.

In past centuries the Earls of Ormonde had done much for the people of their lands, had introduced arts and industries, improved the town of Kilkenny, and built a college in the centre of the town. No rulers had done as much for the welfare and civilization of the South of Ireland as they had done, and Eleanor Butler, a daughter of this great family, could not be indifferent to the welfare of the humble neighbours among whom she was now cast. Both ladies had an affectionate admiration for their " landlord," the decent old farmer from whom they rented their extra land, whose happy married life for fifty years they heard recounted by himself or his wife with so much pleasure. They loved to see the people round about them well dressed, and prosperous and happy, the fields with good crops, the children well cared for. If their garden at times suffered from marauding little boys, after discipline had been invoked, Miss Butler usually intervened to prevent it being applied to their youthful skins. The friends' hearts went out to all birds and animals, and in a period of bitterly cold weather the journal records that they have no real enjoyment of their comfortable house while their fellow creatures and their animals are suffering so much.

The Ladies had two cows, Margaret and Primrose, to which they were much attached, and on one occasion when Margaret was exceedingly ill, their humble neighbours rushed to save her life and succeeded in doing so. The next day " All the village came to enquire about our dear Cow " and the journal records that eight experts were at the moment visiting her. On one

Christmas night the journalist writes: "My Beloved and I got a lantern. Visited our dear Margaret in her stable."

If the Ladies appear to have had an autocratic position, and occasionally to have issued orders, it was only because the valley itself had conferred the position on them for its own good. But so conscientiously polite were they that when on one occasion the local witch wished to kiss Miss Butler's hand, much as she disliked it, she would not refuse her for fear of giving her pain.

The Ladies were regarded as powerful people. A story about them relates that they once intervened successfully to save the life of a man who was sentenced to death. The journal records that an appeal was made to them by a noted sheep-stealer to save him from transportation, but that they saw no reason to try to do so. They received and were distressed by a letter with an appeal from a young woman on trial for child murder. The journal does not say what they did, but they were greatly relieved when a few days later she was acquitted. They believed that if the Judge had read the evidence she must have been hanged on the village green.

In this country life many exciting things happened at Plas Newydd. A wide old chimney caught fire, and again kind neighbours rushed to the rescue, and dealt with the matter. The Ladies rescued a sheep that was almost hanged by some briars; a performing bear paid them an interesting visit. A poor man fell exhausted outside their door and had to be succoured. These happenings were, however, recorded in the journal among events of greater importance. It was necessary to keep account of the stream of visitors who came to them, relatives or family connections of one kind or another, and of people introduced to them, and who belonged to their own world. Through these visitors, Ireland and news of personal friends, and great events in England and France came to Plas Newydd, at times at first-hand. When the journal began, both friends were in their prime, Eleanor, the elder, being so extraordinarily young-looking that the difference between their ages was not noticed. Both were keen, interested, and as sympathetic to younger men and women as they were to people older than themselves. They were good and courteous listeners, intelligent commentators, and brilliant talkers and had plenty to give to, as well as to receive from, those whom they entertained. And, as we know, whether from the highest or from the most humble, there is no hospitality to equal that which is Irish.

Just as Eleanor's journal, in a few touches, described bleak or unfavourable weather, so it records, at times, bleak visitors. As it records the beauty of the day, so it records impressions of pleasant or beautiful visitors. She had a generous enthusiasm for her fellow creatures, and was ready to be prejudiced almost instantaneously in favour of the handsome young men and beautiful young women who came to Plas Newydd. And when describing people of her own kind she had the slight irresistible tendency to gush which is observable in those in whom pride of caste prevails. She did not allow a description to lose as it came from her pen. To contemplate fine manners and elegant clothing also brought much pleasure to the Ladies of Plas Newydd. But they appreciated their fellow-creatures in ways that went deeper than mere appearances, and as, on the whole, they had good judgment, and were moreover entirely without feelings of inferiority or envy, their friendship was claimed and widely appreciated.

Dull or ineffectual neighbours could bore them. There came a neighbour who treated them to a " tedious dissertation on crimes and punishments " and they " wished him hanged for interrupting " them.

They invited the Vicar and found " the good man more stupid than ever." They found another guest " tiresome enough the Lord knows." Lady Milltown and her daughters came and related " Tiresome Royal Anecdotes which I hate."

But perhaps few of us are as generally appreciative as these two very critical ladies were of their visitors. Lady Bellamont was " very pleasing interesting and vastly engaging." Mrs. Bunbury was a " really charming woman blooming and beautiful as an Angel," and they had a " delightful day in her sweet society." Mrs. Kelly was " elderly, very sensible, agreeable, and pleasing." The Bishop of St. Asaph and his wife and daughter were a " most charming and wonderfully accomplished family," and after a much enjoyed return visit the Ladies note that they had " Never consorted with so amiable so accomplished a family." Of Dr. and Mrs. Hamilton and their daughters it was written that they were " without exception the best informed scientific clever people I ever met with."

Their comments on the smart young men who called on them were equally enthusiastic. Arthur Wesley—afterwards Duke of Wellington—was " a charming young man, handsome, fashioned, tall, elegant," Mr. Nugent was " without exception the prettiest young man I ever saw," Mr. Stuart—afterwards Lord Castlereagh—and Mr. Holford were " two charming young men particularly Mr. Stuart who I think beautiful," Mr. Maguire (a relative) was a very pretty young man, tall, elegantly made, sensible countenance. Foreign manners." Thomas Kavanagh, a nephew whom the writer had never seen, was described as " a very pretty young man, genteel person, sweet face, fine hair, very modest," and whom she " embraced with much pleasure." The Comte de Jarnac who stayed for two meals and until 12 p.m. went away leaving them " charmed with him," and regretting that his visit had passed so quickly. Lord Darnley and Mr. Bligh who came were as " kind as ever," while Major Walpole who stayed until eleven was " kinder pleasanter more agreeable than ever. There are few young men of whom we have so high an opinion or a greater affection."

No doubt it was something of an adventure for the younger men and young relatives, who had heard of the scandal of the Ladies' flight from Ireland, to come, or to be sent by their friends, into the stronghold of these two inexorable spinsters, and to find themselves at once laughing and on the most companionable terms, welcomed, rallied, openly admired, or treated seriously by two women who knew so well how to extract their best from them.

"And why," said the brothers Butler, Miss Butler's nephews, to one another, " since they know more about the old country than we do ourselves and seem to love it as dearly, do they not come back? Every one would like to have them! "

In one way or another the Ladies knew a very great deal. Llangollen itself, as a posting-stage, was a centre of news. They received sheaves of letters from Irish or English friends in London or in Bath. They knew all that was happening in Ireland.

In 1789, owing to the illness of King George III, the question arose of appointing a Regent. A number of the Irish peers and commons conceived the idea of inviting the Prince of Wales to be Regent of Ireland, without limitations—as in all respects King. The Lord Lieutenant refused to forward the Irish invitation, but a deputation was appointed, and led by the Duke of Leinster, travelled to London in order to make the offer personally to the Prince.

The Ladies' journal records, on Feb. 23rd, "The Duke of Leinster, Lord Charlemont, Mr. Ponsonby, Mr. Conolly, Mr. Stewart, Mr. O'Neill, all went through the village, having first breakfasted at the Hand, on their way to London to offer the Regency of Ireland to the Prince of Wales. Compliments of the whole party by Mr. Edwards of the Hand to us. Letter from Mr. Ponsonby."

On March 16th, after failing in their mission, the deputation passed back to Ireland, again with compliments from Mr. Ponsonby. The journal remarks . . . " A fine figure they have made on this glorious expedition for the honour of their country."

Possibly these gentlemen, who in their passage to London, or when returning to Ireland, had usually plenty of time for paying their respects to the Ladies in person, sheltered, on this latter occasion, behind " compliments," because, their mission having proved futile, they did not wish to face the humorous gleam which, although struggling with a fixed courteous attention, would have been fairly certain to appear in Miss Butler's eye. Nor did those who were of her family connections desire to encounter the gentle smile of Miss Ponsonby sympathetically receiving the tale of their mistake. When however they reappeared in Dublin and had to confess that pressure of business had prevented their seeing the Ladies they were obliged to evade replying to many pleasantries on their defection.

A few days after this epic occurrence two gentlemen, Mr. Brett, a member of the English, and Mr. Macdonell, a member of the Irish Parliament, dined with the Ladies, and as both took the Ladies' view of the aims of the recent deputation the party made merry over it. But Eleanor Butler presently said: " Acts of violence are not for statesmen."

" But, Madam, was not the invitation to the Prince an act of diplomacy ? Can we possibly call it an act of violence ? "

" Surely, Mr. Brett, if the proposal had been acceptable to the Irish people, no diplomacy would have been necessary. Violence can be done to the political ideas of a people, or a large section of a people by imposing on them that which they are not ready to receive."

It was on the tip of Mr. Brett's tongue to ask who the Irish people—in this connection—might be. Instead, he said didactically: "The idea offered, or imposed, may be a good one, and for a people's good."

"If they cannot receive it, it has been too violently offered, and it may provoke an invincible resistance, and so defer progress. As for your second point we should beware, should we not, of benevolence by force also."

"Your better plan would seem to be——"

"To wait. To educate, and popularize the necessary idea. What we most need in Ireland, but never seem to have, is a statesman who can realize that the country has a political pulse, and who has the gift of touch upon it. In my unfortunate country we never get beyond factions and cliques, and political action is always undertaken at the wrong time. We have a positive genius for that."

"It is hard to wait," the Irishman said.

Miss Ponsonby said, "Parliament itself as well as the people must be led—not jerked into action."

"We might all be dead before we got anything done."

"Oh yes. We might," Miss Butler agreed. "But it is the long view that matters. The creative moment will come when we, or others, have waited. We need the patience of Nature, who does things in her own time."

Mr. Macdonell said, "I do not know that Mother Nature is always as patient as you suggest. In one terrific explosion she can create a new continent."

" She has never yet exploded at the same time, on the same continent, a wise and law-abiding population. When she does that we may have a precedent for creation or even development by violence. But earthquakes are liable to swallow the valuable and the worthless together. If I am not mistaken some valuable members of the deputation will pay for their attempted earthquake."

Miss Butler proved right in her conjecture. The payment was duly made by certain members of the deputation who were deprived of their offices.

As the two men walked down to their inn, the Irish member fell silent and switched the grasses with his cane. His companion said heartily, " A very pleasant visit. I have to thank you for the introduction, Macdonell."

Mr. Macdonell replied " You may! *There* are the women to put heart and patience in a man when he despairs of his country."

" Their opinions, for what they are worth, are certainly sound, although perhaps on the timid side."

" Timid, is it! I would to God we had some sound men of their pattern. I never see that woman without marvelling at her knowledge, and at the ripe judgment of her."

Mr. Macdonell had raised his voice, and seemed to be excited. Believing the theme to be somewhat heady, Mr. Brett said frivolously, " I noticed that the Ladies have a ripe judgment in food and wines. I only wish my wife——"

" If your wife is like mine she knows nothing about either. But you don't seem to realize that you ate nothing except plain Welsh mutton. Its themselves that give the flavour and are the champagne wine. I'd never know what I was eating or drinking in that house—facing eyes like cornflowers——" Mr. Macdonell pulled himself up sharply, and coughed.

To attain an impersonal level quickly Mr. Brett, addressing empty air, wondered how it was that wives tended to lose interest in the things which were their plain *raison d'être*. And why they lost their animation, while single women, even those not always worthy of our respect, seemed to remain so much more lively."

Mr. Macdonell replied in a quarrelsome tone, " I'm a moral man, Brett, and know nothing of the unworthy ladies you name. Excepting for politics, I should be a Catholic. I wouldn't speak of others in the same week with Miss Ponsonby and Miss Butler, but there, as you say, look at those two, as fresh as paint, and brimming with life. Well, they spend nothing, barring meals, on us men anyway."

" One may say it's not quite natural! "

Piqued on behalf of his country-women, Mr. Macdonell snapped, " I believe you. It's unnatural to cultivate a ripe judgment in food and wines to be spent on such as us. What our wives give us is enough for you and me."

" Why, Macdonell, I was only joking."

" Oh, go to hell, Brett, and pick your jokes better. There . . . shake hands with me. No offence, you know. Truth is, the Ladies' coffee

M

has gone to my head. I must go and write to my wife. . . . I'll say good-night to you."

Many visitors introduced the subject of Irish politics at Plas Newydd, only to find that it was not a topic in which Miss Butler was interested. National or local politics, internecine or civil warfare, unpatriotic or seditious scheming for place, position or money, or the buying of votes, were things of which she was ashamed. The idea of really representative government had not yet come to England, much less to Ireland. While both countries dreamed, lacking the conception of political freedom of a genuine character, Ireland bickered, and struggled, and fought, and well-nigh destroyed herself in her chains, and was exploited by both the English and her own Parliament. It seemed to the Ladies that the welter must continue until the fighting Irish factions could crystallize out into a unified body, and until a reformed Irish Parliament should represent the will of the Irish people. But as it stood, the Irish Parliament was a hopeless institution. The commons and their votes were almost entirely in the hands of the powerful families, who had been, and were still, the real rulers of Ireland. Majorities were a simple question of cash payments. Conditions in the country were yearly becoming worse, and the disaffection and fighting were destined to continue until the rebellion, which seemed inevitable, should break out, and, at fearful cost, clear the political atmosphere.

Early in 1791 the Ormonde earldom was restored to John Butler, and his sister became the Lady Eleanor Butler. In 1794 her mother died.

News brought or written to the Ladies was by no means always trivial. When he called upon them, M. de Jarnac related to them all the particulars of the recent capture of the French King and Queen at Versailles. When they were taken to the Tuileries he and his brother, the Duc de Chabot, had been present. He gave the Ladies a long account of this affair.

Again later, their friend Robert Stewart, afterwards Lord Castlereagh and Chief Secretary for Ireland, when sending books to Lady Eleanor Butler,* informed her in his letter of the flight of the French King and Queen and their son from Paris.

The restored Ormonde earldom gave importance to the Ladies, and Plas Newydd became more of an influence on Irish political thinking than its owners imagined. The two friends always with the utmost courtesy avoided any discussion of the motives or intrigues of the great Irish families with whom they were connected, and never allowed the impression to get abroad that Plas Newydd was a centre of political gossip. It might easily have become so, for in their time news having a political bearing was often imparted to influential women in order that their penetrating and voluble pens might broadcast it, and so produce calculated effects in the quarters it was intended to reach. Lady Eleanor was far from believing every one's news, and as to the distribution of news by means of the Ladies, in vain was the political net spread in the sight of any bird at Plas Newydd; Sarah Ponsonby's

* An interesting letter published forty years ago in *Belgravia* and in 1934 in *The Hamwood Papers*.

common-sense and caution could be trusted to see to that. No one went to Plas Newydd with the idea of collecting news, and trusted friends who, knowing the Ladies' warm interest in public affairs, told secrets, were never betrayed. All their own intimate world knew that Lady Eleanor looked for the day, however distant, when a united and liberally enfranchised people under a united Parliament would fulfil the ideals of Burke and Pitt. Because the Ladies were sincere, they were trusted in all sincerity, but among their social equals there were none of the cringing disclaimers of interest in public affairs such as later turned the women of Victorian times into various kinds of imbecile. The men of the eighteenth century expected to have that interest actively shown, whereas the Victorian man decried and crushed it as unwomanly.

In 1794 the Ladies had lived at Plas Newydd for sixteen years. Sarah Ponsonby was thirty-seven and Eleanor Butler was fifty-three. Excepting that they had become more mature in mind, the quality of neither was different from what it had been ten years previously. They were not wilting or hardening, both were as lively and as handsome as ever. People who knew them marvelled at their activity and fine health at a period when so many of their contemporaries, both men and women, were travelling in England, chiefly to Bath or to London, either for the treatment of their gout or rheumatism, or for the purpose of escaping the nerve-shattering disorder and violence which were growing worse in Ireland each year. They still took long walks or climbs in the hills, and were distinguished at long range by their active movement, and by the measured swinging pace which they had acquired in the years during which they had walked side by side.

In winter the Ladies read diligently and studied together. They had already a fine library of the best books in English, French, Italian and Spanish, about half the books they possessed being French. The days of " sweetly enjoyed retirement " could not be obtained very often in summer, when their garden and a round of social gaieties absorbed them, but in winter they plunged joyously into their books for a season.

Following the death of Eleanor's father, there had been quiet mourning in Plas Newydd, unspoken and not indicated save by black clothing. During a period of two years no journal appears. After Mrs. Butler's death a similar, even longer, barren interval is to be noticed.

Those of their own social world who knew that, let separation and sorrow be as it might, a Butler remained for ever of the house of the Butlers, conveyed their condolences to the Lady Eleanor Butler in due form. No person with imagination or the least sense of *noblesse oblige* imputed indifference to the two ladies wearing black habits in memory of the mother of one of them. Indifference to blood or to country in a Ponsonby or a Butler was unthinkable.

In the view of their friends these two charming women, who were so well worth knowing, and whose home was so restful and delightful, must have left Ireland for some good reason. There were a few discerning friends of theirs, for instance Mrs. Powys, Major Walpole, and the Bishop of

St. Asaph, who, contrasting them with more ordinary women, believed that what they had done had been necessary, right, and for the saving of their ardent spirits from destruction. These women were living something of which they others had only dreamed. None of these dreamers could have said what it was that they had dreamed—and forgotten—but dim reminders that they really had dreamed something came to them when the fires and candles illuminated the little dark rooms, or when the Plas Newydd garden blazed with flowers, or as they crossed the field returning under the stars to their inn.

Sometimes friends asked the Ladies if they had no thought of returning to Ireland, and then they looked at one another and laughed, and replied that Llangollen suited them very well. They were sometimes asked whether they would not like to follow their friends to that engaging centre of frivolity and idle gossip, the city of Bath, if only to make more contacts with the world, and again they laughed and said that Llangollen was suiting them well enough. Once, at the question, Miss Ponsonby said with fervour, " God forbid," and Lady Eleanor said: " You see, she knows. Long ago she was there. We do not willingly submit ourselves to such boredom as that would be."

But, whether they would have her or no, Ireland was reaching out to her two escaped daughters, for a grave in distant Kilkenny had something to say to them.

After the restoration of the Ormonde peerage to her son, Eleanor's mother, now Dowager Countess of Ormonde, had left Kilkenny Castle for her dower-house. In the last years of her life

By permission of the Photocrom Company, London

LIBRARY, PLAS NEWYDD

she had lived shelved and lonely, taking no pleasure in her share of the restored honours. She remained to the end refusing to communicate with the daughter who, she chose to believe, had stood in the way of her father's admission to the peerage, the daughter of whom she had not missed hearing as honoured and prosperous, and unrepentant of her chosen free life. Now that her mother was dead Eleanor suffered the pain which is inevitable when the organic tie of mother and child, which survives most lesser shocks, is finally torn away by death. Sarah shared the sharpness of the pain, and carried her own portion of their sorrow.

On a September afternoon they walked for an hour up the mountain road. As they turned to go back home, they began to discuss the book which they were reading over again in the evenings, *Les Mémoires du Maréchal de Richelieu*, but each became aware that the attention of her companion was not on their subject. Sarah especially was looking absorbed, and was responding with difficulty. As they passed under the shadow of a stone wall which bounded a plantation of tall firs, she took Eleanor's arm as though in an attempt to anchor her wandering thoughts. They walked on in silence.

" Look up, at this corner we shall see the sun."

" Yes. Oh! . . . yes."

" What is it ? Say what is in your mind."

" Oh! I don't know," Sarah replied painfully.

" Can it be . . . is it . . . Ireland."

" I believe it is."

" Ireland has taken hold of *me*—most strangely —too."

At the corner of the wall there was a gate, and above the gate they came face to face with the evening sky. It was flooded with green and gold, and striped with narrow burning crimson clouds. They stood still—one did not go just forward without respect in the presence of such beauty.

" Ah! Oh glorious! *Gloria in excelsis Deo !* "

Sarah said, " That too brings Ireland here. But I think the Irish skies carry more clear, more intense colour than the skies over here. It could be by reason of the moisture in the atmosphere over there, I suppose."

" Or the moisture in your eyes over here, my Sally, couldn't it ? Is your heart flying away on those clouds to Ireland ? "

" No . . . my heart is here."

Eleanor pointed with her walking-stick. " The harbour of Waterford is over there. Shall I take you over ? "

" No! To such a bloody land! "

" A lovely land, Sally. With a heart burning within it like this setting sun. We must not doubt that the sun will rise on a purified Ireland . . . some day. Will you go across, just to tell her you won't forget her ? "

" No . . . no——"

" Isn't Ireland pulling you ? "

" Yes. But it is for *you* I feel it. Wouldn't it . . . relieve you . . . to go ? "

" No."

" But . . . it's different for you. I never knew my mother."

" It might have done me good if mine would have consented to it . . . before she died. It wouldn't help me now. One mustn't seek for anodynes. I cannot believe it to be my duty to visit my mother's grave. Mother Ireland has folded her into herself. Your mother too lies in her arms."

" It must have been dreadful for my mother to have to leave her baby."

" It must indeed. And dreadful for my mother to have to leave Ireland and come across the sea after me. She can never have ceased to think of me—any more than I have ceased to think of her. But there is nothing there for you or for me to *live*, Sally. It is lovely of you to share so fully my painful memories. How can I thank you, Sweet Heart."

They rested with their arms on the gate, and watched the heavens in silence for a long time. The sky changed to a deep wonderful blue, but the red clouds like the bloody trails of some great unseen spear lingered in the oncoming darkness.

Sarah said, " I should like to take away from them all the pain they suffered on our account."

"Yes. . . . Will you . . .?"

" You know I haven't words."

And then, as had happened before, Eleanor found the words and Sarah repeated them with her.

" Eternal rest grant them, O Lord, and let light perpetual shine upon them.

" Holy Mary, Mother of God, pray for us sinners now, and in the hour of our death.

(Once more . . . my dear . . . for all of us . . . and for Ireland.)

" God be merciful to me . . . a sinner."

When the friends regained their library Sarah went across the room and stood opposite a little carved figure which they had named Saint Cainneach—the Saint of Kilkenny.

" This trouble about Ireland is your doing," she said to the little figure. " You had no business to be in a Welsh church; you should have stayed over there."

But in whatever manner the trouble had grown, the prayers said on the mountain were heard. The souls of the dead rested afterwards in their Irish soil and allowed Plas Newydd to get on with life.

CHAPTER X

VISITORS

We still have slept together,
Rose at an instant, learn'd, play'd, ate together,
And wheresoe'er we went, like Juno's swans
Still we went coupled and inseparable.
Shakespeare.—As You Like It.

THE letter - writing habit of the eighteenth century persisted into the nineteenth. It was not unnaturally a pleasant habit of the Ladies of Plas Newydd who could never bring themselves to leave their loved home, but to whom communication with the larger world was a necessity. The few women of the day who had a genuine interest in world affairs, books, or ideas, could be sure of a welcome at Plas Newydd. For a time, one of Lady Eleanor's best correspondents was Miss Bowdler, who had opportunities of obtaining news in high places, and wrote her very interesting letters on the King's illness, and other matters of concern to the State.

The Ladies read all the books written by the women of their century, and were friendly with Mrs. Piozzi, erstwhile Thrale, and Miss Anna Seward, both of whom had an acquaintance with friends of theirs in Ireland, and in North Wales. It is evident that all these women understood and appreciated one another. Their correspondence is more than usually fatiguing to the modern reader, who is liable to " wish they would loll a little." Until their style is assimilated it seems so stilted, pedantic and over expressed. It is, however, the medium of expression in which the men and women of their time had grown up, and it expresses balance, good judgment, and the courage to show feeling. Mrs. Piozzi is, on the whole, more readable than Miss Seward, who was a stern guardian of style and English as she knew it. Very different were the letters of some of Miss Ponsonby's Irish correspondents,* who often wielded daring and sometimes scandalous pens, which may have amused the detached Ladies, who, however, were too serious-minded to imitate them. Both Mrs. Piozzi and Miss Seward visited the Ladies on several occasions. Miss Seward, who made their acquaintance in 1795, continued to correspond with them at intervals until her death in 1809, but she was a great invalid and in the end was unable to continue her visits to them. Her accounts of the Ladies, written to a friend, were items of real historical value.

After her first visit in 1795, she wrote to a friend describing their house, their spotless dairy, their garden without a weed, the garden house " with its implements arranged in the exactest order," and the whole scene.

" You will expect me to say something of the enchantresses themselves beneath whose plastic wand these peculiar graces arose." Of Lady Eleanor: " Exhaustless is her fund of historic

* *The Hamwood Papers.*

BEDROOM, PLAS NEWYDD

and traditionary knowledge and of everything passing in the present eventful period. She has uncommon strength and fidelity of memory, and her taste for works of imagination, particularly for poetry, is very awakened and she expresses all she feels with an ingenuous ardour at which the cold-spirited beings stare."

Of Miss Ponsonby: " We see through the veil of shading reserve that all the talents and accomplishments which enrich the mind of Lady Eleanor exist with equal powers in this her charming friend. Such are these two extraordinary women who in the bosom of their deep retirement are sought by the first characters of the age both as to rank and talents. To preserve that retirement from too frequent invasion they are obliged to be somewhat coy as to accessibility. When we consider their intellectual resources, their energy and industry, we are not surprised to hear them assert that, though they have not once forsaken their vale for thirty-six hours successively since they entered it seventeen years ago, yet neither the long summer's day, nor winter's night, nor weeks of imprisoning snows, ever inspired one weary sensation, one wish of returning to that world first abandoned in the bloom of youth, and which they are yet so perfectly qualified to adorn."

In 1797, sympathizing with the Ladies over the illness of their faithful servant, Mary Carryl, she writes: " That she is recovering I rejoice. The loss of a domestic as faithful and affectionate as Orlando's Adam must have cast more than a transient gloom over the Cambrian Arden. The Rosalind and Celia of real life give Llangollen Vale a right to that title."

In 1798 she writes: " For how brilliant a letter in allusive wit and in every sort of elegance am I indebted to my dear Miss Ponsonby."

In the same letter: " I am glad my poem on the future existence of brutes, yet unpublished, has found so much favour in your and Lady Eleanor's sight and that of your friends."

Miss Seward and Lady Eleanor confessed to one another their interest in wild beasts. Lady Eleanor had fed her visitor, the bear, on bread and mutton. Miss Seward had climbed into a booth to see some " laughing hyenas " and was duly thrilled by the " violence" of their noise.

In another letter to a friend Miss Seward writes: " My destined week of elevated situation past, I sought the vale, and swiftly flew three days of high gratification, scenic and intellectual, with the charming Rosalind and Celia of this lovelier Arden."

It is evident that the usually reserved Ladies allowed her to sympathize with their anxieties and troubles. In 1798 she writes: " Our private friends are first and oftenest in our thoughts, beneath the lour of national calamity. I preserve and hear every syllable of Irish news with Lady Eleanor and Miss Ponsonby's image before my eyes, and every hope and fear on the subject passes through the medium of my sympathy with their feelings. Especially since I learnt that their fortunes, as well as anxieties from connection, are at stake in the conflict."

In a very interesting letter written to a friend in October 1799, she speaks of a " four days visit to the Ladies falsely called the Recluses of Llangollen."

"What a little court is the mansion of these Ladies in that wondrous vale! Lords and Ladies, gentlemen and ladies, poets, historians, painters and musicians, introduced by the letters of their established friends, received, entertained, and retiring to make way for other sets of company. They passed before my eyes like figures in a magic lantern.

"This with little interruption is the habit of the whole year, from Llangollen being the high-road between Holyhead and London, and its vale the first classic and scenic ground of Wales. The evenings were the only time in which, from the eternal demands upon their attention, I could enjoy that confidential conversation with them that is most delightful from a higher degree of congeniality in our sentiments and tastes that I almost ever met. Numbers have considered themselves affronted from being refused admittance. I have witnessed how distressingly their time is engrossed by the universal and daily accumulating influx of their acquaintance, and by the endless requests to see their curious and beautiful place, and not seldom for admittance into their company. Beneath indiscriminate admission they never could have a daylight hour for the society of their select friends. They have made an established rule not to admit visits to themselves from any persons, however high their rank, who do not bring letters of introduction from some of their own intimate friends. I have several times seen them reject the offered visits of such who either did not know their rule, or knowing, had neglected to observe it and I always perceived such attempts at introduction pique that pride of birth and consequence of which they have and acknowledge a great deal, eminently gracious as their manners are to those whom they do receive. When the sight of their house and garden only is requested they do not refuse if they are alone, and can either walk abroad or retire upstairs, or even if they have company provided they can walk out with that company, and are not at meals, but it is certain that these impediments to general curiosity often occur, nor has any person a right to think their existence, and the disappointment it occasions, an incivility."

After all, " the Castle is not shown when the family are in residence."

In 1799. " I have to thank you dearest Ladies for a very beautiful but too costly present "—a ring and seal.

That she drew life from Plas Newydd, she shows in 1802 in a letter to both Ladies, for she writes of " those bowers in Llangollen vale whence the purest pleasures have so often flowed into my heart as from a full and over-flowing fountain."

May 1809. To Miss Ponsonby: " Amidst all that carries sweetness to my heart in the letter with which you have lately honoured me, I sigh to perceive its first page shadowed over with the gloom of regret. Justly do you observe, dear Madam, consanguinity and friendship are less often than they ought synonymous terms. When they prove so, separation is very grievous, even though local distance has long prevented the frequency of personal intercourse. The impossibility, the *never never more* is an afflicting consciousness.

" I thank heaven yourself and Lady Eleanor possess in the sense hourly, ocular, and audible, of each other's existence a healing balm for every wound which the resistless dart can inflict on objects of secondary dearness."

Miss Seward had previously written that she believed she could not live much longer, and she died in this year, 1809.

Mrs. Piozzi's appreciation of Miss Seward was whole-hearted. " Nobody has such a notion of her talents as I have." " Her Mental and indeed her Personal Charms when last I saw them united the three grand Characteristics of Female Excellence to very great Perfection. I mean Majesty, Vivacity, and Sweetness."*

To Mrs. Piozzi is owed the preservation of a story illustrating the vastness of the political concepts adopted by one inmate of Plas Newydd. In 1801 she wrote to a friend: " The Ladies at Llangollen enquired much for you. They have more news and more stories than one could dream of. Their best however is concerning their own old Maid Mary. . . . Mary, seeing her Ladies' eyes fix'd one fine night lately upon the stars, said to Miss Ponsonby, ' Ah! Madam, you once showed me a fine sight in the heavens, the Belt of *O'Bryan*, but I suppose we shall see it no more now, since the *Union* '."*

Plas Newydd and its large beautiful garden attracted numerous strangers who were visitors in Llangollen. It was easily reached in five or

* *The Letters of Mrs. Thrale*, Brimley Johnson.

N

six minutes from the village inns, and a field-path
in front of the house gave pedestrians a good view
of its outside. The Ladies, from their garden or
from their windows, had also a good view of
those people who came wandering through the
field in the direction of their door. It was
difficult for ordinary travellers to understand
that Plas Newydd was not a show-place when so
many of their fellow guests at the inns made it
their destination and talked of its charms in the
hearing.

Those of their friends who had once known the
little house, seemed to love to have a finger in its
creation. It was full of books, china, curios,
pictures, and portraits which thése friends had
showered upon it. In the end the Ladies were
presented with more carved oak and coloured
glass than they could use either up or downstairs.
Out of doors, the garden and farm contained
gifts of all kinds—plants, trees, shrubs, cows,
turkeys, fowls, dogs. And while they had to
entreat their friends not to give them anything
more, the Ladies could not do otherwise than
honour the introductions of those who had been so
generous and allow the people they commended
to them to see house and garden. Miss Seward
has shown to what inconveniences they were
put. However, the majority of visitors failed to
satisfy their stringent conditions. Even when
these conditions had been complied with, if the
Ladies did not like the look of the visitors, or
what they knew of the person introducing them,
they were not admitted. But the privilege of
seeing the garden was never refused to the well-
to-do farmers of the neighbourhood, although

By permission of the Photocrom Company, London

OAK ROOM, PLAS NEWYDD

only the superior gentry, or an occasional minister of religion ever saw the house.

Of the rules that governed the nice gradation of claims or the nice distinction in permissions involved in the Ladies' selection of privileged entrants it is not for the teller of this tale to make conjectures. Through long experience Mary Carryl and her understudies had carried out the rules very ably. In the procedure we may be sure there was no inconsequence, no flighty unconventionality. Kings and Princes might condescend to such weaknesses—which were ruinous to dignity—never the Ladies.

All we learn from themselves is through a few permits and refusals which may have been in some way exceptional. Permission was given to the Provost of Dublin and Miss Hutchinson; to "two ungainly maypoles, one of them in the Church," named Watkin; to a large Liverpool party (presumably to see the garden); and to three Miss Williamses "three young ladies in green habits, very fashionable elegant young ladies." A poor wedding-party was admitted to the garden because it was impossible to refuse them on " this probable happiest day of their lives." On the other hand Mr. Walmsley, a London artist, the Dean of Chester's sons and daughters, and three " Creatures without names. Certainly without manners," were refused.

The Ladies had every reason for making rules as to whom they admitted to their house and grounds. Occasionally there were paragraphs about themselves in newspapers, and once the comments were so outrageous that they wrote

to their friend Edmund Burke to invoke his help.
In that period newspapers could make the most
vile suggestions, or resort to open abuse, and for
the victims there was no legal remedy. Mr.
Burke at once took up the matter and threatened
the offenders with effect. In his letter to the
Ladies he wrote: " Your consolation must be
that . . . you suffer from the violence of calumny
for the virtues that entitle you to the esteem of all
who know how to esteem honour, friendship,
principle, and dignity of thinking, that you suffer
along with everything that is excellent in the
world."*

Mr. Burke was practised in doing kind and
helpful actions, and in writing valuable personal
letters to or for friends who were in need of them.
He was himself a man of strong affections and
dependent upon friendship in many ways. When
he was obliged to part with his greatest friend,
William Bourke, who was going to take up work
in India, he invoked the help of Sir Philip Francis
for his friend and himself. He wrote that he
was " parting with a friend whom I have tenderly
loved, highly valued, and continually lived with
in an union not to be expressed quite since our
boyish years. Indemnify me, my dear Sir as well
as you can, for such a loss, by contributing to
the fortune of my friend. Bring him home with
you."†

A man who understood friendship could understand Eleanor Butler and Sarah Ponsonby in all
sincerity; it was with people like himself of

* *The Hamwood Papers.*
† *Memoir of the Life and Character of the Right Hon. Edmund Burke,* by
James Prior. 1824.

simple goodness of heart and capable of fine
human relationships that the Ladies felt an
instinctive sympathy, and in whom they trusted.
They never lacked such friends. When they had
read Mr. Burke's long and wise letter they looked
at one another with serious intelligence.

" Oh, Sally! This kind of thing makes one see
human affairs a size larger."

" Yes. We should have taken his attitude from
the first. How can we possibly have deserved all
the good things he says of us ? Can you think of
any qualities we would like to possess more than
these—' honour, friendship, principle—dignity of
thinking! ' Men like this see in others their own
fine qualities. They reflect themselves upon us."

" He speaks here of our ' valuable lives,' "
Eleanor said. " We—who have only followed the
wild goose———"

" Ah! but, when a beautiful bird flies in front
of us, shows us the way—brings us here—who
wouldn't follow! Why, our bird was a herald of
life. It is our own most special sacred bird."
Sarah threw her arm round Eleanor's shoulder.
" Come out of doors. We might see the very
creature flying over! "

" Going towards Ireland ? "

They laughed happily together.

" Thank God, Sally, the bird did not lead us
to London."

" Nor to Bath. But wouldn't you like to have
a fine flowered dress and go into the world.
You know the world would love to have you—
and I would go that length for love of you,
Sweetheart! "

" You know very well you will never be

tempted. Think of the embarrassment of our Irish friends if we appeared suddenly at Bath!" Eleanor laughed a merry boyish laugh as she thought of it.

"Thank God for our wild goose, Sally!"

"Big, lovely bird! He knew what was good for us. But when we followed him ... what a dark time it was! and how lovely it was when we came out into the light on these hills!" Lovely the hills might have been, but even after all the years that had passed, the memory of the flight that had scandalized all Ireland could bring tears to the subjects of it.

The Ladies' hospitality was occasionally abused, and themselves, in advancing age, mocked by those who had eaten their bread. The innuendoes of Madame de Genlis, and later the odious vulgarities of Lockhart and Charles Matthews, are only to be mentioned that we others may deprecate them. It is with relief that the modern reader can turn again to the polite, old-fashioned salutation of Mr. Burke's letter:

"Mrs. Burke desires her most respectful and affectionate compliments and I shall think myself highly honoured if you continue to believe me with the most perfect sentiments of respect and regard, your most faithful and most obedient and obliged humble servant . . ."

At the end of the century the Rebellion in Ireland was over. The Ladies' men friends and relatives had fought, certain of them had been killed, the houses of others had been burnt or destroyed, fortunes had crumbled. In 1802 Eleanor records in the journal the death of her sister, and of Sarah's half-sister. Ever their

hearts were in Ireland, but the Ladies of Plas
Newydd, whose house was founded on a rock,
continued to live their serene life, and had even
a measure of life to bestow on the young relatives
and friends who could not forget or ignore them,
and who took care that they should lack nothing
that respect and affection could give.

Chapter XI

GROWING OLD

How do I love thee ? Let me count the ways.
I love thee to the depth and breadth and height
My soul can reach, when feeling out of sight
For the ends of being and ideal Grace.
I love thee to the level of every day's
Most quiet need, by sun and candle light.
I love thee freely, as men strive for Right;
I love thee purely, as they turn from Praise.
I love thee with the passion put to use
In my old griefs, and with my childhood's faith.
I love thee with a love I seemed to lose
With my lost saints—I love thee with the breath
Smiles, tears, of all my Life!—and if God choose
I shall but love thee better after death.

THE Ladies had always liked to rise early.
The energy with which they were living in 1807
and for many succeeding years is witnessed by
themselves in their journal. They turned night
into day with considerable frequency, and being
able to afford to drive far afield, (and travelling
was not cheap) they paid little heed to distance
if there was agreeable society to be obtained by
long excursions. On a certain fourth of August
they rose at six, spent many hours in driving, had
several callers, and then adjourned to the sleeping
apartment of a favourite guest where they all sat
conversing until three o'clock. They had just

three hours' sleep that night, for they rose at 6 next day. On the twenty-seventh they set out at 8 a.m. for a long day at an archery match. Later in the autumn they left home on two separate days at 9 and 11 a.m. and returned home on each night at 1 a.m. They once rose at 5 a.m. and went to Oswestry at 6, getting home at 5 a.m. next day. On a Sunday in November they set out at 8.30 a.m., started for home at 12 p.m. and arrived at 4 a.m. On a December day they set out at 9 a.m. and got home at 12 p.m.

In winter or in summer these long visits to their friends delighted them, and there was something Irish orgiastic in these pleasures, enjoyed with abandonment and with disregard of the night. Such inconveniences as frosty roads, sometimes a drunken driver, or the loss of a wheel from their carriage in the middle of the night did not deter them.

At this period Plas Newydd when deserted was well able to take care of itself. In order to relieve Mary Carryl, who was no longer young or strong, as well as to enable the Ladies to entertain their numerous visitors, two able and devoted upper servants were added to the domestic staff. In the absence of its owners the little house full of beautiful and interesting art treasures was shown to visitors under Mary Carryl's discerning supervision a little more often than the Ladies knew of. There was one visit of which she made no report. They were not to be troubled about trifles.

One autumn day a tall elderly man called at Plas Newydd. Mary Carryl, over seventy years of age, wrinkled, spectacled, and less upright than formerly, opened the door. The stranger produced a letter of introduction to the Ladies which he tendered with his visiting-card. Mary Carryl took the card and looking at the visitor began to smile, but checking the smile said, " The Ladies is not at home, sir."

" Oh, I am very sorry. I heard at ' The Hand ' last night that I must come early, and have come hoping not to miss them."

" Sure it's nine o'clock, sir. The Ladies has been gone three hours to Oswestry."

" When do you expect them to return ? "

" I couldn't say, sir. Any time after dark up to the middle of the night." Seeing the stranger's disappointment she added, " Are you taking the coach for Bangor, sir ? "

" Yes, and most unfortunately I cannot stay another day."

There was a pause.

" Er . . . are the Ladies well ? "

" Very well, thank you, sir. Perhaps you might be passing another time."

The tall man lingered on the doorstep. He looked at Mary Carryl. He saw a twinkle in her old eyes.

" I . . . I . . . er . . . You're an Irish woman yourself ? "

" I'm all that, sir. From Ross. Carryl's my name. And I know *you*."

" Why, how do you know *me* ? "

" The last time I set eyes on you, you were dancing the minuet with the Lady Eleanor Butler at the Dublin ball. Would I forget that night tho' it's twenty-nine good years ago. I dressed the Ladies that night for the beautiful reel they danced. Would anyone forget it ? "

" Dublin has not forgotten it. To think that

since then I have been married and widowed, and that night as green in my memory yet, as it is to-day——"

" 'Twas a green occasion, sir. But there was no gentleman of them all was good enough for my Ladies."

" You're right."

There was another pause.

" If you'd like to step in, sir, and write a message . . ."

" Oh . . . er . . . would it be allowed ? "

" Certainly, sir. The Ladies would be sorry to miss an old friend. Come you in."

Mary Carryl knew the effect of the little house upon visitors. She left the stranger at the library table with writing materials before him. When presently she returned he was not writing. He was sitting with his hands clasped on the table staring at the opposite wall. He rose and took up his hat. " Is there a portrait of . . . of either of the Ladies, here ? "

" Portrait ? No, sir. Never a one."

" I won't write here ; it feels like an intrusion. I'll send up my note from the inn."

" There are many that feel that way, sir. If you send it, the Ladies will have it." She handed him his letter of introduction. " You won't want this, sir, until you come again."

" I am glad," said the stranger, but with a question in his voice, " that they are comfortable . . . and happy."

" The angels before the throne of God isn't happier. The Ladies want for nothing, sir."

The visitor pulled himself together and smiled bravely.

"Thank you, Mrs. Carryl," he said. "Will you accept this for the memory that you and I have of the Dublin ball."

He handed her a note for five pounds.

"Sure I thank you, sir. It's a real pleasure to all here to see an Irish gentleman. May God give you long life." She went before him and opened the house door. "If you'd like to walk in the grounds there's nobody about, and you're welcome. Lady Eleanor's own special pansies grows over there."

It is needless to record that Lady Eleanor had no "own special" pansies. But when "on the door," Mary Carryl had watched many men, young and old, leave Plas Newydd. She had observed that some liked to take a flower. It eased the heart.

When the visitor had gone she closed the door, and before she returned to the kitchen folded the note she had received and dropped it in her pocket. "Be the Saints! Another of them!" she said. "Ye'd say the road from here to Dublin was paved with the broken hearts of them! And themselves destroyed with marriage and all . . . and twenty-nine years gone by. . . . Bedad!"

But Mary Carryl was not much longer to be "on the door," nor to rake in the emoluments of the position. She fell ill and the Ladies were no longer able to go afield, but had to see to her nursing. Evidently one immense change was coming to Plas Newydd—they were going to lose her. The Ladies had lost many members of their families, friends, and valued neighbours. New little boys and girls had grown up and had married, and mournful funeral processions from the hill cottages had one by one tramped their way to the churchyard. The restless whirring moth, Mrs. Goddard, had flitted out into Eternity, and now Death was coming to take his toll at Plas Newydd, and to carry away with Mary a great segment of old Ireland.

Mary went away peacefully and in order. The village, which had had numerous conflicts with Mary over the domestic supplies, wept in the church with the two Ladies, and repeated to each other for long afterwards all the beautiful things the Ladies had told them about her, and that she had told them about the Ladies. But far Kilkenny seemed to become very far away now that Mary's emphatic Irish figures of speech no longer rang in her quarters behind the scenes, and the clatter of her high heels no longer sounded on the kitchen floor.

In the midst of their grief Sarah said one day to Eleanor: " Heart of me, ought I to take you to Ireland ? "

" No, Sally. Saint Cainneach settled that before for us, didn't he ? Also I have always thought that the reasons why Mary adapted herself so thoroughly to Wales may have been that she really had the blood of the Welsh settlers in ancient Ireland in her veins. She has never needed nor wanted Ireland, and her spirit may not be there."

" We ourselves might have some Welsh blood. I don't think we can tell. But I agree that we must *not* turn to Mother Ireland whenever someone dies."

" Strange how the desire comes to one, all the

same. Do you remember how you felt long ago
when I went away to London ? "

" Oh! I think not so badly. I knew it was only
for a time. I knew you would come."

" When I have gone away, I shall know you
will come. I shall wait about the door for you,
Sally. It is unthinkable that you will not come.
Show them a brave face, Beloved—for we have
had a splendid life together."

" I will try to do so."

After a few moments of silence Eleanor laughed
an amused little laugh.

" Yes ? "

" I have a feeling, Sally, that when we have
gone away we may be ordered to come back
here."

" As ghosts ? "

" Something of the kind."

" Well, there couldn't be a lovelier place to
haunt. And why would we be limited to Llangollen ? We might have orders to haunt Kilkenny ? After all, ghosts come back not because
of their evil deeds only, but sometimes because
they have been so good—as you have been. If
you come, I shall not need to ask to come with
you—we should be a sort of double ghost! "

Soon they decided that in any haunting that
might have to be done Mary the loving and
faithful ought to join them. For as a result of
saving her wages and of receiving gratuities for
showing their little home for long years, she had
left them the freehold of one of their fields and
five hundred pounds. And Mary had acquired
a faithful friend in Llangollen, one Mr. Richard
Jones. After her death the Ladies gave her

friend a silver drinking-cup engraved with his name and with words in her memory.

It was customary to accompany letters of condolence with memorial rings and brooches, and the Ladies often gave these little mementos to their neighbours who were in grief. Two of these and their accompanying little notes were treasured for 117 years afterwards. Thus, in Miss Ponsonby's fine handwriting:

> Lady Eleanor Butler and Miss Ponsonby shall be much obliged by Miss Catherine Hughes's accepting the enclosed Brooch in memory of the dear Friend of whom it has been the will of the Almighty to deprive her and beg that she will be assured of their very sincere concern on the melancholy occasion.
>
> *Plas Newydd, Llangollen.*
> *8th July* 1818.

and again:

> Lady Eleanor Butler and Miss Ponsonby request that Miss Wynne will be assured of their very sincere concern for the great and irreparable loss she has sustained. She will oblige them by wearing the enclosed little brooch in remembrance of it and of them, and by accepting their best wishes—that her own conduct through life may be worthy of the examples left her by her excellent Mother and Grandmother . . . as it will be impossible for her to live more respectably . . . or to die more lamented.
>
> *Plas Newydd, Llangollen.*
> *6th July* 1819.

Oncoming old age did not prevent their remembering these little courtesies and kindnesses. Two very charming letters from the Ladies in Miss Ponsonby's writing, one dated 1810, the other either 1810 or 1818, that is 117 or 125 years ago, are addressed to their neighbours, Mrs. Williams and Miss Ormsby. They are models of politeness and sincerity, and in their brown old age perfectly to be deciphered, excepting a word here and there.

We are grieved and ashamed Dear Mrs. Williams at having so kind a letter and such magnificent proof of Mr. Williams' and your bounty and recollection in our possession almost four days unacknowledged. But as we trust you will not impute the delay to wilful inattention or a failure in the high estimation we must ever place on any instance of your regard we will only apologize by truly stating that we only received the Packet with its Valuable Contents as we were entering a Carriage for Wrexham where we wished and prayed that some propitious Circumstances might have conducted yours—that we were under the necessity of being back to Dine at Ruabon Vicarage to meet Sir Watkin, Lady Harriett W.W. and Mrs. Mytton of Garth whom we had not seen since her return from the Continent, but for which engagement We should have yielded to the Temptation of prolonging Our Morning excursion as far as Gwenyllt to offer Our thanks in person . . . from that time we have been so occupied with business which would not admit of postponement that this is the very first moment in which we could attempt to present them on paper and assure You in the first place that the Pines are almost the very finest we ever beheld—have arrived at a particularly acceptable season and that we are inexpressibly obliged for them—and secondly that we shall be truly happy in accepting an invitation to Gwenyllt merely to wait on its proprietors—independent of the gratification that we shall enjoy in admiring those improvements of which we have heard so much from so many—if it will suit you and Dear Mr. Williams to admit us before the approaching New Year is very far advanced for We must now be stationary at Home for the expectation of two very near and beloved Relations—on their return from London to Ireland which depending upon the Accomplishment of some particular business we are uncertain as to the precise time of their Arrival here—but should be very unhappy if we had the Misfortune of being absent whenever it takes place—we flatter Ourselves Dear Mrs.

Williams from your not having named Mrs. H——
Sitwell for whose health and welfare our anxiety and
interest continue undiminished that she continues in the
same Comfortable State as the last reports we had on the
Subject led us to trust She was enjoying. We shall be
Greatly Obliged if you can Confirm us in this Agreeable
Confidence—and also by your presenting Our particular
regards and Compliments to Miss Carrie (?) with Our
thanks for the Lupinus Asyanus which She was so good
as to send by the Miss Cunliffes last August, and in very
high preservation—We had hoped that according to a
promise of your bringing her Accompanied by Lady
Broughton to make a second visit we should have shown
her how carefully her gift was attended to. But we shall
rely on that promise being fulfilled in a more propitious
Season as we do upon your believing us with best Compliments to Mr. Williams Dear Mrs. Williams

> Your greatly obliged and affectionate
> EL. BUTLER and SR. PONSONBY.

Plas Newydd, Llangollen.
21st November 1810 (or 1818).

Allow us Dearest Miss Ormsby to remind you of your
kind promise for Monday next and to entreat that
besides the happiness of your own company at Dinner
that day you will indulge us by bringing somebody in
your Carriage if Our friend Miss E. Warrington—or any
other friend of yours should not happen to be with you—
to save us the shame and remorse of asking you to come
so far and return *alone* merely for our gratification—as
though we have a prospect of rewarding You with a little
more spar (?). We are far from certain of Obtaining it so
soon as Monday when we rely upon Your invariable
kindness not to Disappoint Dearest Miss Ormsby's
ever and greatly Obliged and Affectionate

> E. BUTLER and S. PONSONBY.

Plas Newydd, Llangollen Vale.
6 July, 1810.

O

Two letters which Miss Seward would certainly have pronounced replete with " every sort of elegance."

In later years on a cool October evening, the London coaches driving into the "Hand Inn" yard set down two-score guests. Twenty-five of these would only stay for an hour while they had a meal and the horses were changed. But the best rooms were all taken for the night, and when the Bangor coaches had departed some fifteen travellers remained. They would have supper by and by; meantime they gathered in two groups near the large hospitable fires at either end of the old reception hall. Some were friends, some had become acquaintances during their journey. The servants had brought wine, spirits, and hot water, and the guests were enjoying their potations in the agreeable warmth of the fire. The men had removed their hats and great-coats, and were all dressed in the newest fashion in light pantaloon trousers and blue coats. The ladies had retained their outer clothing. A few were in plain habits, but some more fashionable dames, who were not crossing the Irish Sea, were in flowing flowered dresses, poke bonnets with brightly coloured strings, and handsome shawls.

Presently the landlord and his servants brought in cards and dice and put a long gaming-table in the middle of the room, and a group of men, placing themselves round this, began to play. Before he sat down to play one of the men called the landlord and handed him a letter.

" This is for the Ladies; you will see that it is sent up at once. The compliments of Lord and Lady Fitzwilliam and Colonel and Mr. Malone,

ELEANOR BUTLER

and if the Ladies have any commands for
Ireland—the usual message—— See it is correctly
given . . . and, oh! . . . if you are asked how
long we are here say until to-morrow afternoon."

"I will take the message myself at once." His
clientele had thoroughly drilled the landlord in
such polite missions to the Ladies. The sender of
the note resumed his place at the gaming-table.

"May I ask," said an English traveller to the
lady sitting next her, "who these Ladies are? I
am really curious to know; I heard them continually spoken of in the coach to-day, as though
they were great people."

"They come from great families, madam.
Ormonde and Bessborough. They have, I understand, lived in this village together for very many
years."

"Oh! Unmarried?"

"Yes."

"Extraordinary! And they are now old, are
they not? Then what can it be that so charms
our fellow travellers?"

"I have heard that they are very learned, and
have great political influence. I don't know upon
whom. I have never seen them. Here comes
Colonel Malone; let us ask him."

A silence had fallen on the group of men round
the other fire. One by one they rose and came
near to the circle which contained their lady
fellow-travellers. Colonel Malone joined them.
And then the ladies became shy of putting their
question, and looked appealingly at an English
duchess in a large feathered leghorn hat, and she
being filled with curiosity on her own account,
condescended to take the part of interlocutor.

" Colonel Malone, pray tell us why you gentle-men are going to wait on these Ladies ? "

" If they are good enough to receive me, I wish to present my son to them. He has not met them."

It was remarkable how many sons and daughters were introduced to the Ladies of Plas Newydd, but it was a part of its magic quality that it attracted young as well as older people.

Another lady took up the questions. " But does a young man want to know two old women ? And how old *are* they, Colonel ? "

" Let me see. Miss Ponsonby is somewhere about sixty-four. Her friend, Lady Eleanor Butler older—about eighty, perhaps——"

The ladies laughed.

" How do you come to know Miss Ponsonby's age ? "

" All history dates from the year of the Dublin ball."

" Oh, that Dublin ball! We are always hearing how wonderful it was. What happened, Colonel ? Were the old ladies the belles ? "

" They were, madam. No one who was there will forget it."

" Tell us about Miss Ponsonby. What did she wear ? "

" Well . . . I think you ladies might have called her dress pink. I don't know, it was very faint, the colour of her pretty face."

The circle laughed sympathetically.

" Imagine your remembering all that, Colonel! "

" I do remember it. I was just eighteen. We fellows went down before her like grass before a scythe. Such blue eyes! "

" Do go on, Colonel Malone. Tell us more."

" She had long cream gloves and golden shoes, and a . . . and a . . . little feather in her golden hair."

Again the circle laughed delightedly.

" And now, when she's a bent old thing and learned, you're taking your *son* to see her! "

A younger man said, " What *is* the attraction *now*, sir ? "

" Well, young people have dreams. Many of us dreamed. I think that what we dreamed those friends made come true. We rejoice that they are not the failures we others were."

" And what is their success, Colonel ? "

" I will respectfully leave this company to guess, Duchess. With your leave, I won't inflict my eccentric views on them. No one is tolerant of the sentimentality of old men."

A middle-aged man standing behind the group said, " Talking of the Ladies, of course I don't remember it myself, but that ball was their very last appearance. My mother remembered their running away from Ireland immediately afterwards."

" You mean they *went* away."

" No. They ran . . . twice. Caught the first time when one of them broke her leg getting over a wall. The second time your pretty Ponsonby hooked it—in men's clothes. Yes . . . as a groom! Hooked it, and never gave Malone here the chance he was waiting for. They were a thoroughly naughty pair. But you haven't told the ladies about the dance they performed at the Dublin ball—that was what took people by storm. Quite a theatrical turn. Why people began to shout ' Ireland.' My mother said. . . ."

Here, the door opened and an upright old lady entered the room. The speaker dived into obscurity behind the card-players. The newcomer advanced with grace and dignity, and stood for a moment looking over the assembled company. All the men stood up. She bowed and said, " Gentlemen, pray do not let my coming disturb your game." She turned to Lady Fitzwilliam and shook hands. She made an arresting picture as she stood there. Her face had little colour, but was beautiful, with decorative wrinkles round her Irish blue eyes, her thick short hair was white. Her smart cloak hung back off her shoulders, her fashionably cut habit was a shade darker blue than that of the men's coats, her soft necktie was pinned with a golden shamrock leaf, her tall hat became her. The spectators said in their hearts—as poor Captain Moriarty had once said—that she was a Queen.

The circle melted away to the other end of the room, leaving her with her friends. The cardplayers with a desperate effort went on with their game, but somehow everyone was constrained to listen when this old lady spoke, a few tried to watch her as best they could without offence. The four favoured ones sitting with her were addressing her as Miss Ponsonby—the very girl of Colonel Malone's memories. The quiet in the room was more than courtesy demanded, and through it drifted fragments of the visitor's speech.

" Lady Eleanor and I have looked forward to meeting you for a long time. . . . Lady Eleanor would have come with me but I had to ask her to stay at home . . . thank you, she is well, but

SARAH PONSONBY

By permission of the Photocrom Company, London

her eyes have given her trouble lately . . . on that account I have to take care of her. . . . If you will give us the pleasure of your company at breakfast to-morrow morning we shall be delighted to see you all. No doubt you are tired so you must not name too early an hour. . . . I thank you, I must not stay to supper. Now that my friend may not use her eyes by candlelight I am kept occupied, I assure you, and I must finish our letters to go by your coach to-morrow. Nine o'clock then. . . ." She made her adieux and the two elder men kissed her hand. She turned smiling to young Mr. Malone.

" Mr. Malone, would you do me the favour to light my lantern? It is in the reception office."

" May I not escort you ? "

" Will you ? That would be very pleasant."

Young Malone went to light the lantern.

"May we not all escort you, Miss Ponsonby ? "

" No. No! You mustn't hurt the boy's pride—or spoil my fun."

When she had gone, one of the ladies said, " I think I can guess what those dreams are that have come true, Colonel Malone."

" Then you will understand how pleased I am that she has taken my boy with her. I want his dreams to come true."

" But we others cannot understand," said the lady who had spoken first.

Colonel Malone replied smiling, " That is your punishment, madam."

" Punishment! What for ? "

" I do not know. Well, ladies, *that* is the girl who danced at the ball when I was eighteen."

" She is like royalty now."

" She is the same woman, as sweet and good as ever."

" I have never seen a man as far gone as you are, Colonel."

" I am an old man, madam. May I not love an old lady ? "

Out in the darkness young Ned Malone, carrying the lantern, offered Miss Ponsonby his arm. She took it and set their pace in her measured, recollected, almost priestly walk. He was at once struck by the ease and harmony of her steps—generally it was troublesome to keep in step with a woman. He was glad that they were not hurrying. He wished she would talk. He was too well brought up to be clumsy and speechless, only he could not presume to set the conversational pace. But she seemed to know that.

" I suppose you are not yet married, Mr. Malone ? "

" No. Although I seem to be so big, I am only twenty. I suppose they will want me to do it soon on account of the estates."

" Ah! Estates."

They walked on in silence.

" Miss Ponsonby, I would so like you to think me a decent man."

" Because you say that, I do think it."

" I don't want to seem absurd but . . . but when I see what older people make of marriage, it puts me off. I'm afraid of it."

" When I was your age I felt just the same. I used to think that the older people couldn't talk about love and marriage in the way they did if they had ever really known either."

" I don't see why they swear to a thing for life if it is never possible to keep it up."

" I think they imagine they have nothing to do —that it will keep itself up. And we can see that it doesn't. To love takes all we have got. We should never come to the end of it."

" Yet people *do* come to the end."

" I know." They were silent again and then she quoted, as though to herself. " Duty soon tires—but Love goes all the way."

" That's fine, Miss Ponsonby. But . . . does it ? "

" Personally, Mr. Malone, I have found it true. My great love for my friend has gone all the way. And as you see I am now getting very old. And now . . . here is my house door. Will you not come in ? It would give Lady Eleanor so much pleasure to know your father's son."

When young Ned, flushed and bright-eyed, returned to the inn, the company called upon him to give an account of his absent hour. He hated them for it, but he must stand up for the Ladies.

" Come now, Mr. Malone, anyone can see you have had an exciting time."

" There's nothing to say. They were both lovely."

" They! You went in ? You saw Lady Eleanor Butler ? "

" Yes. And if I'd been my own dad long ago I'd have married them both, by God."

The last time we are privileged to take a peep at the journal is in 1821. When she wrote it Eleanor Butler was eighty-three; and although her energy and zest for life was unabated, as

Sarah Ponsonby had told her friends at The Hand, her eyesight was failing. The Plas Newydd library had never ceased to grow and now included several thousand volumes. The years of hard reading by candlelight had told on her eyes, and it was necessary to save what she could of her sight. In this year she records her enjoyment of another Bow-meeting. She never lacked society. Eighty-three could still talk brilliantly, and people still cared to come and listen. The Spirit of Plas Newydd still spoke of life, not of death. Now in their old age both the Ladies could claim that, while they had never for a night slept out of Plas Newydd since they entered it, Ireland had come to them. They had left their country young and in disgrace, mocked by the public, disowned by their relations and friends, the subjects of the most absurd and exaggerated gossip and false stories. They had spoken to no one of their treatment, had asked for no recognition, had not justified or excused themselves, had asked for nothing, complained of nothing. Yet men and women, young and old, crowded to visit them. On comparatively slender resources they answered the calls to entertain their friends, and also the calls upon their strength that long hours of doing so entailed.

The journal recorded some of their days.

On one day: Visitors for luncheon.
Mr. Kenyon, Lady Louisa Harvey, Mrs. Lloyd of Aston, Mrs. Drummond.

To dinner. Mr. Warden of Ruthin, Mrs. Newcombe, Miss Hayman.

Visitors of another day.

Mr. and Lady Elizabeth Kavanagh, Miss Kavanagh, Miss E. Kavanagh, Duke and Duchess of Leinster.

Sunday, August 5th.

Morning. Mr. Lloyd of Rhaggatt, Mrs., Miss and Mr. Augustus Morgan.

To luncheon. Lord Ormonde, Lord Thurles, Lord Maryborough, Lord Burghersh.

To dinner. Lord and Lady Ormonde, Lord Thurles.

To supper. Lady Harriett Butler, Lady Anne Butler, Lady Louisa Butler, Mr. Walter Butler, Mr. James Butler, Mr. Richard Butler, Mr. Charles Butler.

Evening. Prince Paul Esterhazy.

To sleep. Lord and Lady Ormonde.

Surely a strenuous day, August 5th, for eighty-three and sixty-seven.

Next morning: To breakfast and for two hours. Prince Paul and Princess Esterhazy. Their Secretary.

Next day. Lord Kenyon and three daughters.

Next day: To breakfast. Lord Londonderry,* Lord Valletort.

Another day: To breakfast. Prince and Princess Cataldo. Count and Countess St. Antonio.

---

* Son of their old friend Robert Stewart, later Lord Castlereagh, and afterwards first Marquess of Londonderry, who had died four months previously.

Another Sunday: To breakfast.   Mrs. Mellish.
For three hours.   Dowager Lady Lansdowne.
To lunch.   Marquis of Lansdowne, Dr. Hunter.
At 2 p.m.   Lord Wellesley,* Dr. Hunter.

The following incident is related by General Yorke as having taken place when Eleanor Butler was eighty-eight years of age.

" These kind ladies actually brushed the coat and hat of the writer of these lines after a fall from his horse on Dinas Bran Castle in 1827; they also filled his pockets with oranges on that occasion stating that when *they* were schoolboys they were fond of oranges themselves. He was an Eton boy at that time, and their memory is now dear to him."

* Their old and faithful friend, afterwards Duke of Wellington.

CHAPTER XII

SEPARATION

Beloved, thou hast brought me many flowers
Plucked in the garden, all the summer through
And winter, and it seemed as if they grew
In this close room, nor missed the sun and showers.
So, in the like name of that love of ours,
Take back these thoughts which have unfolded too,
And which on warm and cold days I withdrew
From my heart's ground. Indeed these buds and bowers
Be overgrown with bitter weeds and rue,
And wait thy weeding; yet here's eglantine,
Here's ivy! take them, as I used to do
Thy flowers, and keep them where they shall not pine.
Instruct thine eyes to keep their colours true,
And tell thy soul their roots are left in mine.

THE extremely severe and unjust Catholic penal
code made it politic for Catholic priests to get
their education in France, and the Government,
realizing that disaffection was increasing on a
large scale, and that the foreign education of men
of influence was destined in the nature of things
to promote the increase, decided that it would
be better to educate Irish priests in Ireland, and
in 1795 founded and endowed the college of
Maynooth. But laymen and women, the sons
and daughters of the Irish upper classes, were also
often educated abroad. The journal mentions
relatives of Eleanor Butler as having been

educated in France, and tells of one of them who, although the Second Baron of Ireland, could only speak broken English.

Indications of Eleanor Butler's own foreign education can be seen in the journal by her use of French words, and uncertain spelling, and by phrases, ejaculations, or comments of which only one who spoke the language of Catholics would have made use. It appeared unlikely that her Convent teachers had gone out of their way to ground her in the Faith, or to inculcate the strong views on conduct which she held.

Unquestionably the religion of *noblesse oblige* was the real practical religion of both the Ladies, as it is among many people throughout the world. In both, their spiritual outlook and appreciation of finely-lived lives existed parallel with a view of the Christian Churches which, if not entirely uncritical, was exceedingly liberal. Notwithstanding their detestation of the manners and morals of the French aristocracy of their day, of which they had first-hand accounts, and of the revolutionary ideas which had infected Ireland, the Ladies had a great sympathy with the French people and an unprejudiced understanding of rationalistic French thinking. Their years of reading had, in a measure, paganized their Christian ideas, and they were not able to quarrel with nature as much as Christianity demanded they should. Their acceptance of Fate was to them very much the same thing as their acknowledgment of the will of God. In their view anything that was not under the effective control of man existed equally under the will of God or Fate, only God was the more familiar name.

Eleanor's large tolerant acceptance of this God made her kindly towards a world of men who wasted their time in trying to know the unknowable. She often found for herself and Sarah symbols to express what could be, or might be, useful clues to the purposes of God. In Sarah's mind there was a nucleus of glowing mystical feeling which could not be fitted to words, and without Eleanor, Sarah was liable to be inarticulate, self-consuming. Whenever there was something that affected them deeply it was Eleanor who found the words, but when they were found, it was Sarah who made the most use of them, with conviction and relief. Thus it was that Eleanor said Sarah's prayers for her, and thus it had been on a past day on the hillside when Mary Mother of God, understanding Sarah's lack of speech, had come when Eleanor called.

Very occasionally they went to the English churches of the district, worshipping with the most simple piety, and their sympathy with all sincere religion was undoubted, although their Sundays were usually spent in visiting, entertaining, or walking or gardening.

But even Fate may be met in a religious attitude, and they were now engaged in accepting the fact that they were growing old and weak, and in looking in the face the ordeal of their coming parting. Their belief in immortality was not based on the essentially heathen desire to be made one with God, but to remain with one another. They did not dogmatize, but hoped and trusted, as even Rousseau or Voltaire might have done.

After the year 1821, there was no journal.

Eleanor's eyesight became worse and Sarah's days were fully occupied in tending and in reading to her. Eleanor was not allowed by Sarah to miss anything that she could give. Sarah was guide, hands, feet, support, eyes, scribe, and reader to Eleanor. They seemed hardly to be aware that they had acquired the habit of going everywhere hand in hand. Sarah, younger and stronger, made it her care that Eleanor, bent, aged, and nearly blind, should run no risk of accident, and onlookers were moved by her attention to her friend. And still Eleanor was bright and cheerful, and for Sally's sake made no attempt to go up or down stairs by herself, or outside the house to the seat under the trees her own hand had planted, but was docile and thoughtful and unselfish in her blindness, and would not ask Sally to do for her what others could do as efficiently. When she was eighty-four doctors came and went, and came again, and the great surgeon Alexander decided to operate in the hope of giving her sight. There came a dreadful day when all the household except the patient was sick with anxiety and solicitude and the operation was performed. After it was over they were told with what fortitude she had borne it, how she had never once flinched nor moved an eyelash, and how obediently she had responded to the surgeon's orders while he worked. She did not even lie in bed afterwards. She was wonderful and the doctors hoped they might see good results. The hillside was proud of her and boasted of their Lady's courage and endurance. For a long time afterwards friends and neighbours from the little mountain houses, and from the village, found excuses to come at all hours to the kitchen door, to bring gifts and to ask how she did, because all the valley wanted to know. Passing along the field-path, they could see her in her armchair, her head on a white pillow, and Miss Ponsonby reading or writing by her side. The labourers and men of the lime-kilns lurked about behind hedges hoping for news. Then the white pillow disappeared and her own merry laughter was heard again. Next, in due time, she walked in the garden on Miss Ponsonby's arm, and then Miss Ponsonby sometimes beckoned to a favoured mortal to come and speak to her invalid, and the visitor received her own assurances that all the pain was gone and everything going well. Later, when the news went round that her Ladyship's spectacles had arrived and that she might now see better, the whole valley rejoiced.

The current John Jones, gardener, said to Jane Hughes, the head maid, " Look you, books won't tempt her Ladyship nor yet flowers won't tempt her. It will be Miss Ponsonby's eyes she will be seeking when she has her own again." " And proper too," responded Jane, " What else, I ask you, would her Ladyship spend good sight on ? Not rubbidge like you and me, nor books that can be read to her, nor flowers that she can hold in her hand and have the scent of them. But we mayn't hope for too much, Mr. Jones—spectacles isn't eyes."

Eleanor Butler had long envisaged the problem of how Sarah might fare when, with her own death, the chief part of their joint income would disappear. With characteristic pride and independence they saved what they could, and

P

Eleanor's long life had enabled them to reduce their problem to manageable proportions. Sarah would have enough money to carry on Plas Newydd, and Eleanor knew that she would leave friends who would stand by Sarah in her extreme old age. Sarah, herself an old woman, had but one anxiety and that was to outlive Eleanor. She knew she had not Eleanor's exceptional strength and was convinced that she would not long survive her friend.

Their property was worth several thousand pounds and after money had been left to their two faithful servants there would probably be a little for a residuary legatee. Their choice, for which they each had reasons, fell upon Lady Betty Fownes' granddaughter, Caroline Hamilton. As Eleanor saw it, long ago Sir William Fownes had done an unforgivable thing; he had coveted and had made a scandal in connection with the young girl Sarah Ponsonby under disgraceful circumstances. The girl had defended herself in a spirited letter* threatening to leave his house and tell his wife and daughter of his conduct and had been obliged in the end to leave his house. A copy of her letter and of some subsequent notes, which Mrs. Goddard had seen, also lay in a cabinet at Plas Newydd. These constituted every evidence as to what long years ago had occurred. Defence of Sarah's honour had not been possible then, but the Ladies even in old age were not given to making mistakes. They knew what had to be done. Eleanor intended that one day, even if after any number of years, Sarah's action and her own part in it,

* See page 276.

as two honourable members of great families, should be justified to posterity.

The scandal which had reached both Mrs. Goddard and Lady Betty's daughter, Mrs. Tighe, had been cut short by Sir William's sudden illness and death, the runaways were safely out of Ireland, Woodstock was now owned by Mrs. Tighe, the past could be buried. The past, however, was not buried, for in Mrs. Goddard's diary it was entered that " Sir William told me before *Mrs. Tighe* his illness as I said was his own fault that he was punished for." And the diary also described Sarah's final scene with Sir William, of which Mrs. Goddard had been a witness.*

Mrs. Tighe's daughter Caroline Hamilton, their intended legatee, was born a few months before her grandfather's death. She was twenty-one years younger than Sarah Ponsonby and thirty-six years younger than Lady Eleanor Butler, and never saw either of them until Lady Eleanor was at least sixty years of age. She was a smart fashionable woman of the world, who should be able to survey the facts conveyed to her impartially. But she already knew the story from her mother, and in her short occasional visits to the two old ladies she made no reference to buried history. When they were gone the dead would have effectively buried their dead. To the Ladies, however, who felt that their lives were about to end, Caroline was the obvious person to whom to bequeath their evidence. On a still summer's day they sat in their garden with their papers before them, Sarah writing, Eleanor holding, but not attempting to read, the sheets of small fine script written fifty years previously.

* See page 277.

" I don't know, Eleanor. It is a very long time ago. Two generations are gone. Could you expect a third to rake up their grandfather's errors ? "

" If they have any pride of family or understanding of what becomes ladies and gentlemen would they not wish to do so ? You know them best, Sally. You think they will not do it ? "

" Caroline is her grandfather's and her mother's own child. I think she will not do it."

" I, too, think she will not do it. Then she will have to tear up these letters."

" If she were to choose that, would she not tear some of the skin off her own soul ? " said Irish Sarah.

" I should not mind that. It might do it good. I have no idea of your carrying their family sins into eternity."

" Very well." The deft-handed Sarah pinned the letters together and tied them again with their old faded ribbon.

They duly made the bequest to Caroline Hamilton and Sarah wrote out the draft of the letter which would inform her of the fact.

As they sat later under the trees taking their coffee, Eleanor reflecting on their morning's work said :

" I am glad we have preserved and left Caroline those papers. I feel strongly that that family will not succeed in covering up the truth for ever, Sally. If Caroline does not tell it, some other generation will."

" If enough time is allowed to pass, descendants are liable to become proud of the weaknesses of their ancestors. I may become in the future the beautiful Miss Ponsonby, breaker of all hearts. Seriously though, Eleanor, with what patience you await the fulfilment of our story! It is only comparable to your patience over Ireland. But what contents me most is the hope that we shall be able to leave to that family the little bit of money that was spent on keeping me at Woodstock. Then we shall be clear of it."

How would the Ladies have felt if they had known that more than another century was to pass with the truth still concealed! Or what would they have said if anyone had prophesied to them that in a hundred years' time the great house of Woodstock, which had been the scene of Sarah's persecution, would be non-existent—burnt to the ground, its splendid demesne demolished, and Sarah's story told.

When Sarah returned to the garden she asked Eleanor, " What are you smiling about ? "

" I am thinking that one would like to die in all respects as a Lady of the very best quality should."

That in the end was easy. There came a day when the Lady Eleanor could not take breakfast and seemed to wish to sleep. The two faithful maids were with her while Miss Ponsonby took her breakfast below stairs. And then Elizabeth ran down stairs and called her to come. And not ten minutes afterwards, clasped in Sally's arms, Eleanor slipped away. And somehow the watchers below, as well as the two standing back at attention in the little upper room, felt that fluttering exit that was not stayed by closed doors. Sarah came to her two companions and said calmly, " Everything is well, my dears. She is gone, but I do not think death has been in this room. Let us all do what we ought. Go now and call the people to us whom we need. The doctor . . . Mrs. Evans . . ."

*   *   *   *   *

The laying of Lady Eleanor Butler in her last resting-place, close to the door of the village church, was the most impressive scene that had taken place in the valley in the memory of living man. None of her great friends, English or Irish, were summoned. Nevertheless the inn yards and roadways were thronged with the carriages of her wealthy neighbours, and church, churchyard, and ways of approach, were overflowing with rich and poor, many of whom had come long distances. All awaited the coming of Eleanor Butler to do her the last honours. All were taken by surprise when she came. In that time funerals were black, and pompous, and rather ridiculous. Ladies were seldom in attendance, or were present laden with crape and hidden in black veils. A funeral was a terrifying affair. There was nothing correct about this burial, yet it did not lack pomp and circumstance. The wistful feeling of the simple people of the hillside had been told to Miss Ponsonby, and she had invited their help. A long procession came over the field from Plas Newydd and down the lane, bearing the bier of their Lady covered with a splendid pall of garden lilies and all other summer flowers, the work of many hands. Behind came the old lady whom all knew and loved, in her black habit and loose summer cloak, leaning on her stick, but with firm deliberate step. Her two servants on either side of her carried more flowers.

This chief mourner's face was sweet and tense —absorbed; but she had no tears, no veil, no trappings of woe, for this burial, as she had made her helpers understand, was a triumphal procession—the formal passage of the Lady Eleanor to God. It was the people who lined the roads, who, looking on her beautiful handiwork and her aged, attentive face, shed tears and sobbed as she passed. None of the many gentlemen who would have come forward to assist her had an opportunity of doing so. She passed with the body of her friend into the church as though no other person existed.

Eleanor had loved music, and there was good music for her to-day. There was a service but Sarah did not hear it; she seemed to herself to be in a place between two misty worlds. Only two or three times did sentences reach her hearing, and each time she and Eleanor had answers to them. When the music had faded out, she heard a voice proclaim, " We brought nothing into the world, and it is certain that we shall carry nothing out." The voice she knew replied to her, " Excepting ourselves, Sally, and a love that has not failed."

Yes—and was that " *nothing* " ?

By and by a voice was reading: " And that which thou sowest, thou sowest not that body that shall be, but bare grain it may chance of wheat or of some other grain. But God giveth it a body as it hath pleased him and to every seed his own body. All flesh is not the same flesh . . ."

Ah! but yet how people who thought they knew

tried to limit the unknown undreamed-of purposes of God, as though some kinds of flesh could not be informed by spirit! Again came music, purifying speech, and then again the praying voice—" that we . . . may have our perfect consummation and bliss both in body and soul in thy eternal and everlasting glory." What! something so complete that nothing more could be desired or obtained ? Was not that only a way of describing death. . . .

Then she was at the graveside and the service was over. People were waiting for her to move away. She looked at her companions who came forward and laid their flowers in the grave. She took her own bunch of flowers and let it fall softly into the grave. As she stepped back, a rough half-bred collie dog ran in front of her and throwing up his head began to howl. The sound startled and disturbed the waiting crowd profoundly. The dog howled again and she spoke. " No! No! Don't drive him away ; he is keening the dead. Poor dog! are you lost ? Come then . . . come with me." She shook hands with the clergyman and with the group of friends round about her. She smiled as she refused a great man's request to be allowed to drive her home.

" Thank you . . . no. This is Lady Eleanor's day, and as you know we have no carriage. Any other day I am at home and glad to see you and your wife." Passing through the lines of people she shook hands with a few, including whole groups in her thanks for their presence. At the gate she shook hands with a very poor old man and woman. " Lady Eleanor would have loved the beautiful flowers you brought her, and your

kindness has made such a difference to me."
Then to her humble assistants, "How can I
thank you all; it would have been a sad day for
me without your help." And now she took her
walking-stick, and passed up the slope to her
house on the arm of her maid, the dog following
close behind her.

And the crowd, moved and astonished, said,
"That is what it is to be Ladies." Others said,
"Ah! blood tells," which is what Lady Eleanor
had always believed, too.

Once at home again, the two servants, seeing
Miss Ponsonby's fatigue, made haste to care for
her; it was so long since she had allowed herself
to rest.

"There's a little fire in the library, ma'am, we
thought you might be chilly. Wouldn't you come
and sit in your chair ? "

"I will. Lizzie, go and get the dog a plate of
meat and some water. As he seems to have no
owner we will keep him here."

"Yes'm. Leave her cloak on at present, Jane,
and take off her hat and shoes. I'll go and get a
glass of wine."

"Thank you for all your goodness, my dears.
I'm tired of course."

"A cushion for your back, ma'am, and a
footstool." Jane knelt down and removed Miss
Ponsonby's shoes. The old white hand rested
on the girl's shoulder. "You're both so good.
I shall be all right."

"Here's the dog's dinner, ma'am. And I've
brought you a little sip of rum in hot water and
a finger of cake. Try it, ma'am. It will warm
you."

" Here are the slippers. Cover her knees and feet well, Jane. There! Now, ma'am, you'll rest. Ring if you want us, here's the bell at your side."

" Yes," Miss Ponsonby said absently. " I keep hearing that music."

The servants retired and closed the door. The dog, having eaten, gave a sigh of satisfaction as he lay down at her feet.

" You're right," Sarah said to him, " all is well."

In a few minutes Jane opened the door, whispered " She's asleep," and closed it again.

Strange that the music Sarah had not heard as she left the church, now came beating into her brain. She recognized it as a funeral march, but it was as soft as a cradle song. It carried one with it—walking—walking—Now it faded out. Now it was no longer a march—it was sparkling music, light and rapid. A drum was tapping briskly, the music was whirling, she was dancing in a brilliant green dress and white vest. The tune grew louder and louder. Then came a silence— and a burst of applause—they were cheering for Irish freedom.

The dance music had died out, but the beat of soft marching went on—softly—softly—she was tramping to its rhythm with a lantern on a long road in the dark, going to meet—to meet—O passionate first fruit of liberty! Sarah started in her sleep and half awoke—and received the sword-thrust of reality. What! Nothing ? " Oh, good-bye, Eleanor. Good-bye." But the voice of the one who was with her answered, " Not good-bye, Sally! There is no such word for you and me in any world." She rested again. The beat of the music was now the tiny slap of water on the sides of a sailing-boat which leapt over the wavelets and carried them before the wind over an unknown sea. Now the beat was in the air. And above and before them, in level unerrant flight, the wild goose was leading the way.

(See Note, page 277)

PART III

THE LADIES MEET ME

Chapter XIII

THE FUTURE ARRIVES LATE

When, as they come springing up into consciousness from our inner and underworld, attractive or terrifying people approach us, whether they are expected, whether they appear to belong to a past, to the present or to a future period of time, we should make the very most of the experience. These people do not come to us for nothing, and if we ignore them may never come again. We should receive them with courtesy, should not be so foolish as to question them, nor so futile as to ask ourselves whether they are the material of dreams or visions, or are ghosts or spirits, nor should we begin to talk of illusions or delusions or of what is real or unreal. We cannot expect to have answers to enquiries on such subjects seeing that we do not know what we are ourselves, nor whence we came, nor where—if anywhere—we are going, and it is only ridiculous to ask for information from strangers. When we have the good fortune to meet these people we should be perfectly simple over it, take them as real, approach them on what they indicate is their own ground, and try to meet their desires. If we are reasonably, or even unreasonably, friendly, we may make for ourselves satisfying friends—or foes. I who write—obscure, matter-of-fact, elderly, sceptical—have in the course of my life acquired powerful friends after meeting them in most uncanny circumstances. Not only this but I have seen and talked with gods. And as at any time one only meets with parts of people —or of gods—one must take what one gets in a thankful spirit.

If you will observe the above elementary rules I can assure you that you will never have to complain that your results lack incident, intensity or profit. But if you only fear what is uncanny, or begin to argue or run away, you may be chased; and being chased is hurtful to personal dignity.

When last year I went, in response to a dream of Vale Crucis Abbey, to Llangollen where I had not been for fifty-six years, I met the Ladies of Llangollen, who had then been what is termed dead for 103 and 105 years. I went to look at their house, which now belongs to the town, that is, the town thinks it owns Plas Newydd because it has paid good money for it. At the time of my visit I did not know the Ladies' real history, nor of their delightful journal, nor what a small chance I should have had in their lifetime of seeing their interesting house, which is now empty and desolate. Nor did I contemplate the possibility of their being still, for just as long as they choose—Town Council or no Town Council—in possession. At any rate no one could have been more surprised than I was, when, as I entered the house door, I had at once an overweening impression of their invisible but actual presence there. I felt very much embarrassed, and like a vulgar intruder who had no right at all, even if I had paid a shilling for the privilege, to be there or to be looking at their rooms and handiwork and relics.

Being there in the room with them, I could not run away. I could only hope that since I was in their presence they would understand how apologetic I felt, and how confused. But somehow, almost at once, I knew that I was not unwelcome, that they wished me to be there, and that they were aware of my presence and would like to say something to me. They followed me all over the house, either by my side or close behind me, and once seemed to stand, so that I could not pass, while I looked at an old watch in a little case of relics.

I went out of doors and they followed me all over the garden. In the past they must have taken large numbers of visitors into their gardens, and they seemed anxious that I should see everything. I stayed there because I felt they desired it. Although we were thus in one another's presence for about two hours, it is amazing to me now to remember that I never tried to look at or speak to them, nor they to speak to me. It was the most vivid and remarkable experience I had ever had in my life, but nothing at all came to me through sight or hearing. This vivid impression remained with me for many weeks afterwards.

During the following winter I read the Ladies' Journal, and a number of books or papers written up to the present day which all repeated in some form or another idle or malicious conjectures and irresponsible statements which had for so many years constituted their only " history."

Q

About eight months later I visited their house again, but on that occasion they did not seem to be there. I had an intuition that they could not be very far away, and I stayed in the town for some time and occupied my days in exploring the neighbourhood. In a hundred years the town had of course grown and changed a great deal. Many landmarks and plantations were not as they were a hundred years ago. Only the church and the hilltops had not changed, nor the stone on their grave, which remained as they had placed it. The hills drew me to themselves, and one morning I was impelled to walk on that hillside where 130 or 140 years ago they had gone almost daily for " our accustomed walk."

In her journal 147 years ago Eleanor Butler had written " Rose at half-past six. The loveliest blue and silver morning I ever beheld." At such an hour on such a morning, I became wideawake and was drawn towards the accustomed walk. The day promised to be very warm, but the white mists of the night's cool breath were still floating upwards to be dissolved on the hill-tops. To climb the mountain side I chose a very gradual ascent on a green path, and proceeded slowly with the aid of my walking-stick, for now that I am old the slightest ascent is for me a climb. As I went, I became suddenly expectant and felt sure I should encounter the Ladies— not however at once, for I could see all over the hillside on which I was walking for a great distance. All the same, I was convinced that they were near—possibly again invisible, possibly following me. I listened for any sound of movement or for rustling in the short bracken which covered the turf. I kept looking round about me and above and below, almost fearfully, although in the expanse before me not so much as a stray sheep was to be seen. I exhorted myself to be ready, not to be taken by surprise, not to be foolish, and not by any means to neglect to speak aloud as soon as I was assured of the Ladies' presence. Once only I halted to take a little breath, and then turned to face the morning sun which was striking the tops of the mountain range on my left with a fringe of gold. I stood for about half a minute enjoying the beautiful effects of sun and shadow, and then turned to continue my walk. I had gone about twenty paces when I was suddenly startled by the short bark of a dog, and there, only a dozen steps away from me on the open hillside, seated with their feet upon the path, I saw the Ladies. Why I had not seen them sooner I cannot imagine, the very suddenness of their appearance was in the last degree astonishing. Just at the moment I saw them they turned their heads and appeared to see me. They were sitting so still that I thought they were in some kind of sleep, but in a couple of seconds they seemed to wake, and touched one another as if to call attention to my advent, and peered at me as though they were uncertain of my reality. I halted in my advance so that they could look at me, and in the course of about ten seconds I had a good look at them. There was no stamp of either youth or old age about either, for such states have little to do with the larger personality that comes of life vigorously lived in its prime. They were strong, healthy, experienced, refined—ladies to their finger-tips. They wore no head-covering and their hair was turning grey. Their faces had a curious serenity, were stamped with a beauty not of form or feature, but of spiritual achievement—something they had attained. They wore habits of cool light blue linen fastened up for walking, showing fine muslin inside their short open jackets, and dainty white petticoats below their skirts. At Miss Ponsonby's feet lay the rough dog, " Chance," who had once followed her to the end of her days —and after. It was he who had seen or heard me first and had barked, and he now lifted bright eyes to mine and thumped the ground twice with his tail. I saw Lady Eleanor Butler start as she looked at me, although she at once controlled the surprise she evidently felt at my likeness to her friend. Well—here we were, able and ready to converse with one another. Time for us was not abolished, but it had become plastic in a curious inexpressible way, and in order to reach one another we seemed to slip for a season into the fourth dimension.

As I came the few steps towards them, they stood up and turned to me. I must have impressed them favourably in spite of my clothing of Shetland homespun and my strong brown shoes and rough stockings. They looked at me with kindly interest—I knew that they would be capable of describing me afterwards as " a very well behaved person—considering——"

" I believe," I said, " that I have the honour of addressing Lady Eleanor Butler and Miss Ponsonby."

" Yes! You must excuse us that we do not know to whom we are speaking, nor to what circumstances we owe the . . . the pleasure . . . of this meeting."

" Neither do I know why we are meeting. For my part, I believe I am somehow ' called ' to it, therefore so I hope you may be."

I spoke with suave politeness which I could see affected them favourably.

" How can we serve you, madam ? "

" I will try to explain if you will be good enough to afford me a conversation with your-selves—giving you, of course, my name and credentials first."

" Oh! Have you——"

How habit persists from world to world!

" Yes," I replied. " I have an introduction which cannot fail to be satisfactory to you. May I offer it ? "

" If you please." We were all smiling pleasantly.

" To begin with my name is Gordon."

" Oh! Are you——" Lady Eleanor stopped, puzzled.

I laughed and said apologetically, " Plainly, I could not be anyone you have ever heard of. I came into this world too long after you for that to be possible. But when the Butlers were buying wine for kings, the Gordons were taking other people's beverages away from them and drinking them themselves. Long before there were any English kings the Gordons were accomplished robbers."

Lady Eleanor burst into a joyous chuckle.

" I have only a great-great-grandfather and he was a well-to-do Lowlands farmer. My name is Dr. Gordon."

" *Doctor!* did you say ? "

" Doctor. I may write seventeen letters after my name. That's *my* title. And I'm not the kind of apothecary's apprentice who looked after the health of the ladies of the eighteenth century. Something altogether superior. But now for my introduction. Some months ago, you and Miss Ponsonby introduced yourselves to me and took me, together with a fairly large public, into your confidence."

They were too polite to seem to question what I said, but Lady Eleanor turned to her friend and said:

" How did we do that, Sally ? "

" We will ask you to tell us if you will be so good," Sarah Ponsonby said.

" Certainly," I replied. " But I keep you standing. Without prejudice to your being able or not to endure me later, may we not for the moment sit together on God's own hillside."

I was extremely careful. I remembered social distinctions, and when they had resumed their seats I sat down in a lower place opposite to them, the dog lying between us. They made a deprecatory gesture, but I could see I mounted in their estimation.

Looking up at them I said: " Some months ago I bought from a bookseller a large book which contained the " Journal of E. B. and S. P., written by E. B."—" the short and simple annals of the poor——"

Miss Ponsonby said: "Good Heavens, Eleanor, did I . . ." and Lady Eleanor smiled and shook her head reassuring her.

" With it were published many other papers

which you could never have seen—a long time
has passed."

I paused. They had forgotten their journal,
and my news recalling it was evidently a shock to
them. They were feeling stripped and robbed.

"Would you be good enough to inform us,
madam—Dr. Gordon—when and how our
journal reached the public?"

"It was published a year ago. That is all I
know about it—and that was about one hundred
and fourteen years after its completion. But you
know you lived in an age of diaries . . .
memoirs . . . autobiographies, and of much
letter-writing. They were no doubt relieving,
but were dangerous diversions. On the whole
one may marvel that your journal lay hidden
for so long." I saw that they were still feeling
outraged that the dear intimate record had thus
been exploited.

"Don't think I don't understand your feelings
about this. Twice in my life writings of my own
have been stolen and published. But when you
left your journal to the wrong person, did you
not inadvertently give it to the world? If one
lets intimate documents go out of one's keeping,
the world, which is a damnable devouring shark,
is bound to get them in the end. Why should
your journal be immune from the fate of most
other journals?"

"True, why indeed."

How reasonably they were accepting a fact
that pained them more than they yet knew, but
already deeply!

Anxious to soften the blow I had inflicted I
said, "It may be good to realize that in your

own library were dozens of memoirs and autobiographies—such histories seldom contain much
truth."

" Such as they were they were of human
interest—about remarkable people," Lady
Eleanor said.

" And so was the Journal of E. B. and S. P.
We of to-day think you something more than
remarkable. You can take to yourselves the
credit of having given to posterity something
really valuable."

" How could that be ? "

" Your journal has no word in it that you
need regret having uttered. Personally, I was
moved by its quality, its simplicity, truth, sense
of honour, appreciation of human values, and
by the beauty of life it connoted. I am as pleased
to have seen it, and known you in it, as I am to
be considered even a trifle like Miss Ponsonby."

" I am afraid we cannot look upon our handiwork—this thing that is our own fault—as
favourably as you seem to do."

I hoped it would not occur to the Ladies to ask
me what the world had said about them in the
days between their lives and mine—the days
especially accursed for women of the Victorian
reign; I had more to tell them. The theme of
memoirs seemed to me a good one on which to
harp.

" I have seen a list of the books you left at
Plas Newydd," I said. " In your library you had
twenty-four books on religious subjects, a very
modest number out of several thousand works.
Whereas you had twenty-six on gardening—a
goodly number. But I counted seventy-two—

you must have had many more—by or about
women. It is plain that you cared about the
subject."

"Yes," Miss Ponsonby agreed meditatively.
"We bought all we could get—we thought the
world of women was not on the whole a happy
world . . . we felt for . . . some. We dreamed
of a better world."

"Sometimes," I said, "it seems as though all
the truth in the universe lies in dreams—and it is
lovely when the dreams come true. Can you
remember the first idea that charmed you when
you were quite young ? "

At this question their interest increased.

"Why, the idea of individual freedom," they
said together.

"It was the same with myself. I would have
died rather than not have had my freedom to
do what I liked with my life. I required my own
life. But I doubt whether much truth is to be
obtained by accounts claimed to be authentic
of other women's lives. Not much has been
obtained through others' accounts of yours.
And after all, when we have read everything we
can get about them, what does anyone of us
know, for instance, about Madame de Genlis,
Madame d'Orleans, Ninon de l'Enclos, Madame
de Maintenon, or all the rest. As much has
probably been imagined about them as about
yourselves. But in your journal the truth comes
crystalline. It is as though you had been born
and had lived together in . . . in a . . . in an
amethyst. But really as things have turned out,
are you not thankful that you wrote your own
journal ? "

" Are we thankful, Sally ? We ought perhaps to be thankful."

" You ought indeed," I said. " Look what you left out."

They both laughed confidently and Miss Ponsonby, caressing the dog's head, said gently, " It is all a long time ago. It doesn't matter any more."

" There is a tremendous lot of Fate wrapped up in Time. You have been gratuitously depreciated and slandered for a hundred years." They winced —their feelings were more acute than their serenity indicated.

" You," I said to Miss Ponsonby, " were once young and undefended."

" In the end we left it too late. So many of our own people died, there was no one . . . we trusted to Caroline," Lady Eleanor said.

" Caroline Hamilton failed to respect yourselves or your wishes. She had your money and things and your journal. She herself wrote a journal. In it she told your story, but said no good word for either of you. What had she to write about— she was only born in the year in which you left Ireland ? In her journal she repeated idle and unpleasant gossip. She did not spare you or your family, Lady Eleanor, nor did she justify you as against her grandfather, Miss Ponsonby.* Her journal was a despicable production. If there was ever anything meaner than Caroline Hamilton's conduct in respect of yourselves, I have not in a long life come across it."

I saw Lady Eleanor's blue eyes blaze and brim with tears.

* See page 278.

Sarah Ponsonby, smiling, said again, "It is a long time ago. What do we care?"

"No," Lady Eleanor said. "We don't care. *I* feel it for my friend, but we don't really care any more what they did."

"You might forgive and forget but might still carry a sore place a century old. But I would like to tell you that you had one witness who gave a true account of the circumstances of your leaving Ireland, a witness whose naïve sincerity is unquestionable. She also left a diary——"*

"Not Mrs. Goddard!"

"Yes."

"Mrs. Goddard—who was so cautious—of all people!"

"I don't say that Mrs. Goddard intended to defend you from being thrown to the wolves; indeed it was her detachment that served you so well."

"With her horrid nonsense about Eleanor's debauched mind?"

"Forgive her everything, for she described your final scene with Sir William."

"Oh!"

"You don't wish to see this evidence I speak of which the world now possesses?"

"Thank you. No. We think not. It is impossible to care beyond a point. We ourselves have not always been just——"

Their old feelings might have remained, but their old life had evidently become impersonal; they could not care about it. They had never lived while on earth entirely on one another to the exclusion of their individual interests, and I

* See page 279.

wondered and would much have liked to ask them what they were living on now. But that would never do.

" Would you allow me to ask you a question ? "

They did allow it, and I said: " Have you searched for me ? "

" We have certainly looked for someone. For some months we could not find anyone. We felt you—but we couldn't see or hear you. We are most grateful," Sarah Ponsonby added, " that you came to tell us these things. They will make a difference of some kind to us, we believe. But you must have more than these things to tell of."

A silence fell between us—such a silence as only occurs between people who have considerable harmony of feeling. Although our conversation was laboured and tentative, it was something to have found that we could converse, apparently with profit. We remained silent for about a quarter of an hour. Miss Ponsonby meditatively stroked the sleeping dog. I hypnotized myself by plucking and staring at the centre of a small yellow flower. When I looked up Lady Eleanor was leaning forward looking at me with a challenging amused smile, and seemed to be more like the lively creature she had been in her past days. She read the eyes of her friend and then turning back to me she said, " We think we ought all to pursue the implications involved in this meeting—as far as may be. Do you feel that you could talk freely ? "

" Not only can I, but I greatly desire it, if my modern speech is not too strange to you."

" You have the advantage of knowing our

history. In meeting you we are in the presence of something that we need—something new—will you try to convey it to us. You have said that we are separated by a period of Time. Can we bridge over the separation ? "

" I do not know—but only by doing so shall I obtain the peace of soul which the Journal of E. B. and S. P. has taken from me."

" We did not know we had been sleeping. Now we feel there can be no movement for us until we have caught up with the century we have missed —we did not know that it could be such a misfortune to lose count of Time."

" And not know precisely where we are in creation."

Lady Eleanor explained. " Miss Ponsonby has always liked to know her bearings; that is why once she drew so many maps of the world."

I replied, " Dates are not my strong suit. I too tend to slip out of Time. But we will make an effort to retrieve ourselves."

Remembering their very exclusive attitude I said, " It appears to me that . . . point of view is as important as Time. Have we anything there in common ? Am I to be allowed a stringent attitude towards your ideals which are really my own."

" Oh, surely. If we have conveyed anything else, forgive us."

I said, " We shall clear a lot of ground if we make that plain."

Lady Eleanor Butler, her eyes dancing and her mind full of interest said, " How are we going to define Ideal ? "

" We don't define it. We symbolize it. As a wild goose—or any other white bird."

" A wild goose *chase*? " she asked, puzzled.

" No. The bird itself."

" Could you say more about it ? "

" I suppose it could appear—as it were—' a Dove lighting upon Him.' "

The friends looked at one another. I wonder if I had not been present, whether—— And what depths there were in Sarah Ponsonby's eyes!

Beaming on me she asked, " You are a poet ? "

" Other people ask me that when I use some poor symbol. No. I assure you, no. But I ought to go away now. Can you say when and where we should meet ? "

" Oh, if it is agreeable to you, at Plas Newydd. It is so quiet there. At about a quarter to ten in the evening to-morrow."

" Thank you. I will be there."

It would be impossible to describe the amazement and confusion of mind in which this encounter left me. I, who had never troubled myself about the question of survival or immortality of either the man or the soul, now fell into the need of a fresh orientation in the light of my experience. For here in Llangollen was a tomb in the churchyard, and here on the hillside the Ladies had laughed and talked with me. And where was I to place myself. I was not far from the end of a long and full life. I was the same age as Sarah Ponsonby had been when she had—gone away. A few more years was all that with luck—for I did not want to die—I could expect. And then what ? Change. Would it be the kind of change that had come to these two, and should I acquire the impersonal view of my own past history which they had acquired towards theirs ?

I considered their life. They had lived it intensely. They had dreamed and struggled and had suffered the loss of homes, relatives, and country. They had been made a laughing-stock to the common people, and the opprobrium of their proud and jealous social contemporaries had smitten them. They had been wild, people said, and had disgraced their order and birth. They had plunged into circumstances which it had required all their own pride and the greatest courage to overcome. Yet their names had lived when those of grander, more powerful people had vanished into the obscurity of the smallest type in *Burke's Peerage*, where you had to look for them. They had created a partnership full of duty and responsibility and had left behind them a fragrant atmosphere of well-doing. They had lived long and loved ardently, and now when they had passed the grave and gate of death they had an impressive beauty and dignity even if they might perhaps have been a trifle more human. How had it come about that they could haunt their former surroundings without the least distress—able to feel deeply but no longer caring. How was it that I had been " called "—as I had phrased it—to come and look for them after a space of say 150 years in which we had needed one another, had been possibly dependent upon one another—they on me that I might give them back some lost coherence in whatever their present life amounted to, I on them for the renewal of my little bit of remaining life, such as it was ?

Surveying myself—rapidly ageing, somewhat tired, with not very much more that one could live if one tried—I had to admit that the past had largely fulfilled itself, high obstacles had fallen flat, pain was blunted. Probably I should travel to a point at which I would not care what happened to me. Was it the mere circumstance of death that had enabled the Ladies not to care— to wander indifferently on their loved hillsides, or about their dismantled, decaying, ghostly little house, the house that had been for fifty years their pride and joy and in which they had lived happily and died with fortitude? Was it death—or good dying—that had reconciled their active minds to forgetfulness ?

Presently I was beset with the notion that I, myself, was somehow the actual cause of their return. They had slept away their hundred odd years until the interest I had taken in them had roused them to come back, seek me out, desire to question me. They had got far—for Lady Eleanor had said they realized that there could be no movement for them in their present life until they had redeemed—had assimilated—that hundred years. And now something was " up to me."

Well—God help me—I had lived seventy-five years out of the hundred they had missed, and should have to invoke their tolerance, their charity, their wisdom, while I unfolded the detestable tale of my own experiences. As I thought over my life, it seemed to me that I was the blackest object that ever spoilt the end of the " loveliest blue and silver morning " in a beautiful place.

CHAPTER XIV

THE WHITE BIRD

As clouds sweep over the moon
The hosts of the dead pass by :
They veil the terrible face,
The inviolate face, of the sky.
They fill the winds of the world
With the sound of their gentle breath:
They temper the glitter of life
By the merciful shadows of death.

Evelyn Underhill.

WHEN one is bound by space and time, it is not particularly easy to keep an appointment in a place from which the public are carefully excluded at night. At Plas Newydd I had locked gates, iron railings and bolted doors to negotiate.

I laid my plans early in the day after carefully surveying the possibilities. I am cut out by nature for a burglar, but as long as I remain in the flesh I must not incriminate myself; therefore I propose to conceal the details of the way in which I broke in in order to keep my assignation with the Ladies. I made haste, for by the time I had effected my entrance the moon was rising. I made my way through the rooms in order to be sure that I was alone in the house, taking off my shoes when I mounted and descended the stairs, lest the custodians who lived adjacent to the house

R

should hear me. As I passed through the ante-room that led to the library, the gilding and the colours on the old Spanish leather on the walls were beginning to glint, and it was lighter still in the library. This long room was almost empty of furniture, but it contained a very old high-backed sofa and two carved oak chairs. I pushed the sofa further into the shadow at one end of the room. I examined the window at this end, and found that I could open and escape through it, if need were. I sat down on the sofa to await the Ladies' arrival. I thought I might receive some soft summons to admit them, possibly to guide them in by the way I—but never mind that.

On most week days tourist sightseers swarmed over the house, generally ignorant of what they were looking at, mocking it, or expressing dis-appointment that there was in their opinion so little to see. How different was this evening in " our peaceful delicious cottage." After fifty years of such quiet, was it wonderful that the Ladies in the extended peace of their changed life had overslept themselves and were even at this moment not up to their appointed time. I remembered with interest those timeless excur-sions of theirs in their later life on earth, from which they might arrive at home at four or five o'clock in the morning—it seemed as though they had even then been detaching themselves from Time. I went on listening for small noises. In any ordinary house, there are creakings and crackings and ghostly thumps, for we all know that things become animated and walk about in the night. In my own house, the grandfather clock is often taken with inner rumblings and

THE DESERTED HOUSE

then flumps up the stairs and comes to my
bedside, but he does that because I live usually
in too much dependence upon him, and he likes
to pretend to me that he is something other than
a timepiece—I do not know what—his pranks do
not deceive me. But in Plas Newydd there were
no noises—the silence was absolute. Indeed the
silence would probably strike as much horror in
some of my friends as would noises, were they to
spend their night hours in this cave of shadows,
alone, or with ghosts. This house was both
serene and intensely aware. I have seen enough
of death to note that its calm often looks full of
wakefulness, but I did not imagine that the calm
of death was the calm that was over this place.
Rather—oh, most welcome idea—it was the calm
of life well and fully lived—of satisfied achievement. There was nothing over which the house
needed to groan or creak. I gave myself to the
quiet which was so intense that it became to my
acutely attentive senses almost a noise in itself.
I sat watching some squares of bright light which
the moon was throwing on the floor at the other
end of the room, and presently closed my eyes
and I must have dozed a little. I dreamt I heard
doves cooing in the trees outside the house, and
when I looked upon the room again it was lined
with bookcases and held several tables on which
were piles of journals and papers. In this setting
I saw Lady Eleanor Butler cross the room and
take a book from one of the shelves. I started to
my feet and realized that I had been dreaming,
for the room was empty of books, and Lady
Eleanor was not where I had seen her two
seconds before. Both ladies were standing close

beside me and greeting me with quiet satisfaction, but in the subdued voices that belonged to the night.

I stepped noiselessly across the room and carried one of the oak chairs into the shadow, and next I was seated on the sofa beside Lady Eleanor, while Miss Ponsonby sat on her left in the chair so as to face us. They said how much pleased they were that I had come. They seemed to me to be more awake, more expectant, eager, and human, and more at their ease with me than they had seemed to be on the hillside yesterday.

I felt that I was something more than a well-behaved person now, and I bestowed on the Ladies my brightest smile of good fellowship.

" You have accepted me," I asked, " as an infamous but impenitent thief of your acquaintance through your journal ? "

Lady Eleanor laughed a rich jolly laugh.

" Yes. And we desire in return to know you. You do not suggest to us that you are a thief of anything."

" What do I suggest ? "

" Tell her, Sally, my dear."

" Something . . . very strange to us . . . yet . . . which ought not to be strange . . . something beyond us . . . yet belonging to us. . . . Something that we *must* have——" Miss Ponsonby spoke slowly with great difficulty.

" Then will you let me clear a path for myself that I may come to you by it. We have already agreed that the greatest thing in the world to us is freedom. Possibly the subjects of those memoirs on your shelves felt in the same way "—I waved my hand towards the empty walls. " I suppose all those women lived and loved and suffered and died, and were cowardly or brave and were unduly praised or blamed for being what—perhaps—they were not? But we three regard many of them, do we not, as having been slaves."

" Yes, because they dreamed of freedom and would not take it."

" I dare say they thought they could both wear economic chains and be spiritually free," I reflected.

" Well, everything pressed very heavily on them."

" But you women of the nobility in the eighteenth century were much better educated than others, or than those who came after you, and you had a good deal of . . . not freedom, but licence. As far as I can understand that time, you were all expected or expected yourselves, especially you of the noble families, to marry, and all regarded yourselves or were regarded as failures if you did not."

" Here were two who did not accept that."

" I know. I have never married. I understand. But it came to this: that the world said a woman's condition was an unchangeable quantity predestined for her before the foundations of the world. Whereas a man's destiny was what he chose to make of it. The Church has proclaimed a married ideal, and on that all our social laws are based. That marriage seems to you a reasonable and proper contract ? "

Lady Eleanor said : One is entitled to have a high personal ideal, and if it cannot be realized to decline to make the contract. One should live what one believes—*we* did."

I said: "Faithful husbands are doubtfully common nowadays. I gather that in the eighteenth century they were as rare as black diamonds."

"That is so. It was not expected."

"And divorce was very rare. And I understand that wives and husbands condoned one another's misconduct to a considerable extent. No doubt for the sake of family succession it was thought better not to make destructive scandals."

"Yes; it was rather dreadful. It led to much that was very painful for one or other party to bear. Slave women, as you name them, accepted it. We could never have submitted to that condition of things."

"If one is to be a *Lady*," I said, "one must not only act as one but must insist on being treated accordingly."

"Why that, of course! Oh, of course," they said.

"Your ideals have always been my own—personal worth, honour, integrity. But if marriage could not be counted on to secure what it demanded because something called human nature was always denying it . . . then . . . well . . . anything else did as well ? "

"Or something else—friendship—did a great deal better."

"For us. Women in our position have generally had enough money to enable them to follow their own path. But for all the rest, in your time and after, if they forsook or were forsaken in the prescribed path they could be left quite without means of support. That was the whip-hand over them. They had no money, and no means of earning any. If a woman walked away from her husband, she did not walk to freedom when her only alternative was to sell herself to some other man. The economic position of women in the first half of the nineteenth century became worse and worse, and their longing for freedom and justice greater and greater. Out of these two factors have come the cardinal changes in women's lives."

" Changes do you say—really changes ? "

" Changes which have made a woman like me so strange to you, yet here we are talking together as I am fairly sure you never talked to your great friends. And now, think only of these things that have all come about during my lifetime. The law of divorce is equal as between men and women, and either can easily obtain a divorce for due cause. The property of every married woman and all her earnings are her own. The obstacles placed in the way of her earnings are almost all removed. Marriage is still not understood nor sufficiently seriously undertaken, but no woman has now to submit to slave conditions, and no woman who is not a born slave does so."

" How wonderful all this is ! "

" There is much more." How was I to tell these two about the last hundred years ? It could not advantage them to hear of Queen Victoria, of the Chartist riots, the Indian Mutiny, the Ashanti, or South African or Great Wars. Nor of Mr. Gladstone nor Mr. Disraeli. Nor could I expect railways and radio and battleships and aeroplanes to interest them. They had passed out of this kind of history. What they were missing and seeking was to adjust themselves to the life and thought of the women of this day—their own future in Time—for their personal relations with the present were suspended, their old life had become impersonal and without living relationship. As Lady Eleanor had said, there could be no movement for them, and there could be no real waking from sleep while what should have been their own immediate future remained outside their cognizance. They had also to understand the New Man. If only I could have placed the works of George Meredith and Robert Browning and Maurice Hewlett on their shelves as a beginning!

" Am I speaking of what you wish to hear," I asked.

" Yes. Do please continue."

I told them of the changed economic conditions which had made it increasingly difficult for the growing populations of our countries to live, of the difficulty for parents of supporting their large families. Of the excessive numbers of the women, of the severe repression of their desire to work, of their lack of education, finally of their abject poverty, which in my own day had resulted in widespread prostitution, destitution and disease . . . how I myself had found women (and the best educated among them), almost starving. Then of their beginning to rebel, of the uniting of all classes of women in a demand to have the parliamentary vote. Of their gallant platform propaganda, of their demonstrations, and imprisonment with its ill-treatment, and of their final triumph. The eyes of the Ladies were burning like stars in the dim room as they drank in what I related. " And now," I said,

" when every boy and girl over twenty-one has a parliamentary vote, and votes cannot be bought——"

" Oh, my God! Sally! Imagine if Mr. Pitt and Mr. Burke had been there to see the last of their dreams of freedom come true! As she faced the moonlit window, I saw the tears run down Lady Eleanor's face. This tale was bringing her back to life; she was not dead, but sleeping.

" I wonder," I said, " how Mr. Pitt and Mr. Burke would have taken the scene in the House of Commons the night our Franchise Bill went through."

" You were there ? "

" I was in the vestibule. The galleries were so full I could not get a seat. We were tremendously touched by the way the men who were in our favour rushed out of the lobby to tell us. I wouldn't have missed it for the world. Now, women can be Members of Parliament and Cabinet Ministers."

" Oh! Eleanor! That's where you should have been——"

" Should be, Lady Eleanor," I corrected.

Then I told them of the women in the Great War, of the Dames of the British Empire, and of the position of women in universities and professions . . . and then I paused for a rest.

" It is as though you were describing the world from the top of a great staircase."

" Then climb it with us and be on a level. I need not say you will find it safe. Heaven is not up our staircase."

Miss Ponsonby presently said: " It is rather hard that many women on account of their numbers cannot marry when the conditions of marriage are now so much better."

" It is better for the country, is it not, that the women should be in the majority? The curious thing is that they don't seem to find not being married always hard. After all, if a woman is the marrying kind she does marry. If she has not the genius for it she is better not doing it. No one thinks it remarkable now if two friends prefer to live together. They do so all over the country. You two friends would be no exception nowadays."

" And poor working women ? "

" Some poor working women choose it too."

" We understand that our friends said some rather awful things about us."

" Never Irishmen! But nothing like as awful as people afterwards said about us. We modern women do not ask advice; we have had enough to last us for centuries to come. We do as we think good. We have a women's club in London with this motto: ' They say—What say They ?— Let them say! ' "

" You think married people are happier than they were ? "

"Unquestionably. But there also have been immense changes in their conditions. Devices have been popularized which enable married people to avoid large families. Only very exalted people for economic or family reasons, or very poor people, have more than a few children. A great many married people do not want to have any children at all, and do not have them. They have of course no reason for finding fault with the friendships of women which are from the point of view of population no less sterile alliances than their own——"

" What, as a doctor, do you think about it ? "

" As a doctor, nothing. It is not a question for me at all. But as a student of natural science, I think that, when such a powerful instinct as the parental instinct chills down to zero, Nature has her own good reasons for the phenomenon. A phenomenon which coincides with other changed conditions but is not, I think, a result of them. But a child should not accidentally choose these people as parents."

Silence fell between us again, and after a long pause I said, " A writer on such subjects has reminded his readers that children of the spirit can be of more value to the world than children of the flesh."

Lady Eleanor's large serious eyes rested on my face. She took her friend's hand and held it.

" Miss Ponsonby and I are finding all you say incredibly good news. It is enough to upset any old-fashioned people like ourselves. You must pardon our being affected by it."

" You must not think that we achieved what we did without blood and tears and great sacrifices. We suffered from family quarrels, from social bans, and from mockery, contempt, discouragement, every kind of brutality from both men and women. There was nothing that you two suffered from your friends that some of us did not suffer too. We have paid for what we have. Lives, health, happiness were given generously on the altar of freedom by women far more heroic than I could ever have been. But we should be ungrateful indeed if we did not remember the men who stood by and helped us by encouragement, defence . . . votes . . . money. . . . Those men were splendid friends."

" Will you tell us of your own life."

I sat thinking about the task. Then I said: " If we are to speak of personal griefs we will do it to one another only. As I said yesterday, look what you left out of your journal; you showed an exquisite taste; and even in our present lives . . . well . . . an imputed superiority obliges one . . ."

" How well you understand us! What of your doctor's life ? May we hear ? "

I described to them the preliminary and medical curriculum, the years of hard work and what it all meant.

" You were happy ? "

" I was not unhappy. Men and women were my book. It was a concentrated experience of human states and motives."

" You couldn't have liked it."

" Would anyone like cutting up dead bodies for the best part of two years ? Or doing post-mortems among the flies in a hot London August; or learning operative surgery on the dead ? Would anyone like treating filthy, infected, verminous people, or criminal, drunken, half-sane people ?—we had no nice rubber gloves in those days—our bare hands. The battlefield is not an agreeable place, but it is there that the bits must be picked up.

" Ugh! Horrible! And to think of our soft luxurious life, Sally."

I said, " After a time one became accustomed to anything. One did not waste good feeling on sheer ugliness. There was plenty of pathos on which to spend it. But you know what it has taken me seventy-five years to live through, cannot be told in five or six hours—I am especially glad to be able to refer back to the eighteenth century in order to record my acknowledgments to it."

" Wasteful, unbelieving cynics that we were! "

" No, no. There were pioneers to whom *we* feel infinitely grateful. We have sometimes told them so."

" Oh! May we ask who those were."

" Your two selves, for instance! "

" Ourselves! Just consider our lives! "

" Just what we have been doing ever since we knew you through your journal and saw its total incompatibility with anything that had been said about you. And before we had that, you were there for us. Is it nothing to have shown the world a perfect love . . . to have shown it in your darkest times . . . to be showing it now after a hundred years ? That was indeed doing your bit. Had you any idea how many women have been on a pilgrimage to this little old house of yours ? Silently, saying nothing to anybody—but they came. A girl of seventeen came once. She is here again in her seventy-fifth year."

" But what did we *do* ? "

" You made the way straight for the time that we inherited. You meditated among your books and dreamed us into existence. You handed on to us your passionate love of freedom plus honour. We may very well ask our spiritual progenitors how we, discouraged and belittled as we were, came to be born as we were. People like yourselves are the answer to that. You can go away and dream again now—if you must—I myself shall soon be in that sleep too. But sleep implies waking."

"What," Lady Eleanor said, looking at me solemnly, "is the resurrection of the dead ? "

" I do not know. But it seems to me to occur. If you look at our old churchyards, how quickly the headstones get overturned and lost. Something upheaves them. They symbolize something that cannot hold down the soul. If you keep a grip on Time I am ready to believe that you two may come here again. I think you have immortality, which is another matter from mere resurrection. It is life everlasting. But I do not contemplate that for myself. I haven't earned it. Oh! I hear your neighbour's cockerel, practising his crowing. Here too is daylight. If I don't vanish at once I may be caught, and the Town Council would have me put in prison. This night would have been worth it; but I had better go. Would you be so good as to close this window after me ? "

As Sarah Ponsonby held the window open, a gust of cool air blew in upon us. " The wind of the Spirit from the wings of the white bird," I said, smiling at Lady Eleanor. " It is the Spirit of new birth. Will to be born. Come again."

I passed one leg out of the window and sat for a moment astride the low sill. Sarah Ponsonby stepped up to me and looked at me with a deep solicitude.

" You ought to write the poetry that is banked up in your spirit," I said, smiling up at her.

" And you . . ." she said. " Have you no
one . . ."

" To call me Beloved . . . and go with me ?
No one. I thank you for your sweet concern.
But one must not quarrel with one's own share
of the price of our freedom. Good-bye."

THE LADIES' GRAVE, LLANGOLLEN CHURCHYARD

(*The triangular Gothic stone enclosed by railings*)

APPENDIX

Three Inscriptions on the Tomb of the Ladies in the Churchyard of Llangollen Church

In Memory of
MRS. MARY CARRYL
Deceased 22nd November 1809

This monument is erected by Eleanor Butler and Sarah Ponsonby of Plas Newydd, in this Parish.

Released from earth and all its transient woes,
She whose remains beneath this Stone repose,
Steadfast in faith resigned her parting breath
Looked up with Christian joy and smiled in death.
Patient, industrious, faithful, generous, kind,
Her conduct left the proudest far behind;
Her virtues dignified her humble birth
And raised her mind above this sordid earth.
Attachment (sacred bond of grateful breasts)
Extinguished but with life, this Tomb attests,
Reared by two friends who will her loss bemoan,
Till with her ashes here shall rest their own.

S

Sacred to the Memory of

The Right Honourable

LADY ELEANOR CHARLOTTE BUTLER

Late of Plas Newydd in this Parish

Deceased 2nd June 1829

Aged 90 years.

Daughter of the Sixteenth Sister of the Seventeenth
Earls of Ormonde and Ossory
Aunt to the late and to the present
Marquess of Ormonde.

Endeared to her friends by an almost unequalled excellence
of heart, and by manners worthy of her illustrious birth,
the admiration and delight of a very numerous acquaintance from a brilliant vivacity of mind undiminished to
the latest period of a prolonged existence. Her amiable
condescension and benevolence secured the grateful
attachment of those by whom they had been so long and
so extensively experienced. Her various perfections,
crowned by the most pious and cheerful submission to the
Divine will, can only be appreciated where it is humbly
believed they are now enjoying their Eternal Reward,
and by her, of whom for more than fifty years they constituted that happiness which, through our blessed
Redeemer, she trusts will be renewed when this tomb shall
have closed over its latest tenant.

" Sorrow not as others who have no hope."
1 Thess., Chap. 4, v. 13.

SARAH PONSONBY

Departed this life on the 9th December 1831
Aged 76.

She did not long survive her beloved companion, Lady Eleanor Butler, with whom she had lived in this valley for more than half a century of uninterrupted friendship. " But they shall no more return to their house, neither shall their place know them any more.—Job, Chap. 7, v. 10.

Reader pause for a moment and reflect, not on the uncertainty of human life, but on the certainty of its termination, and take comfort from the assurance that " As it is appointed unto men once to die but after this the judgment: so Christ was once offered to bear the sins of many; and unto them that look for Him shall he appear the second time without sin unto salvation.—Heb., Chap. 9, v. 27-28.

NOTES

The letters and extracts quoted in these notes appear in " The Hamwood Papers " by Eva Mary Bell (Macmillan)

Ch. IV, page 77

LETTER FROM SARAH PONSONBY TO MRS. GODDARD

" At first I believed it almost impossible for so professed a man of honour to throw off the mask so shamefully and that my prudence would secure me from appearing to understand him. But be satisfied that neither my pride, resentment, nor any other passion shall ever be sufficiently powerful to make me give Lady Betty any uneasiness in my power to spare her, and I sometimes laugh to think of the earnestness with which she presses me to be obliging to him for I have adopted the most reserved mode of behaviour ever since (Taking no pains, when she does not perceive it, to show my disgust and detestation of him). I would rather die than wound Lady Betty's heart."

Ch. XII, page 226

LETTER FROM SARAH PONSONBY TO SIR WILLIAM

I desire to be informed in writing and only in writing whether your motive for behaving to me as you do is a desire that I should quit your house. If so I promise in the most solemn manner that I will take the first opportunity of doing it, and that my real motive shall ever remain concealed.

If not, I require the most solemn assurance from you, that you will never directly or indirectly address any language to me which Lady Betty and Mrs. Tighe might not hear and approve of. I further desire to know if you would wish me to inform them of what you have already honoured me with ? Be assured that my conduct towards you has ever been dictated by the most innocent gratitude and respect, and I appeal to your conscience if it is possible for me to preserve them now. Suffer your vanity to be silent for a little time and you will judge whether it is possible for me to feel any other sentiments towards you.

Ch. XII, page 227

EXTRACT FROM MRS. GODDARD'S DIARY

Sir W. joined us, kneel'd, implored, swore twice on the Bible how much he loved her, would never more offend, was sorry for his past folly that was not meant as she understood it, offered to double her allowance of £30 a year, or add what more she pleased to it even tho' she did go. She thanked him for his past kindness but nothing could hurt her more or would she ever be under other obligation to him. Said if the whole world was kneeling at her feet it should not make her forsake her purpose. She would live and die with Miss Butler, was her own mistress, and if any force was used to detain her she knew her own temper so well it would provoke her to an act that would give her friends more trouble than anything she had yet done. . . .

Ch. XII, page 235

SARAH PONSONBY'S DEATH

Miss Ponsonby died eighteen months after Lady Eleanor Butler. Her dog, " Chance," disappeared on the day of her burial, and was never seen again.

Ch. XIII, page 250

CAROLINE HAMILTON'S JOURNAL

Mrs. Caroline Hamilton in her journal writes of Sir William's conduct:

"... *though his daughter was married and had children he still lamented that he had not a male heir, and believing that Lady Betty was in a declining state of health he fancied that the time was approaching which would leave him at liberty to marry a young wife. He had a pretty face, he thought, and was not much above fifty. In this disposition of mind he cast his eye on Miss Ponsonby after she had lived in his house a year or two. My mother told me that he was suspected of treating her with too marked attention, and she, willing to excuse her father, thought that more was imagined than was intended, and I, his granddaughter, charitably wish to think the same.*"

But Caroline Hamilton's charitable wishes were to no point in the face of the fact that she *knew* the truth.

"*Be that as it may Miss Ponsonby during her own life never mentioned the subject to anyone.*"

Caroline Hamilton had Mrs. Goddard's Diary and knew that Mrs. Goddard knew everything, and that by Miss Ponsonby's request she had told Mr. Izod about it.

"... *but after her death I found copies of some notes to him* (her grandfather) *carefully put by in a pocket book.*"

That is all! Not a word of what the letters to Sir William were about—Caroline Hamilton's descendants might as well have believed that they were love letters from Sarah Ponsonby.

"... *and I found letters from her to Mrs. Goddard complaining about her unhappiness.*"

Not a word as to what had made Sarah Ponsonby unhappy.

Ch. XIII, page 251

MRS. GODDARD'S DIARY

It is not known who Mrs. Goddard was, nor when her death occurred.

The last time she appears in the Ladies' journal is in 1789. She would then be at least seventy years of age. In the following year the journal records that Mrs. Goddard's great friend, Mrs. Rogers, in deep mourning, visited the Ladies and took away with her some legal paper. Three months later they wrote out some request to be dealt with after their death, sealed it, and placed it in a certain drawer of their desk. We know from Caroline Hamilton that Sarah Ponsonby left her all her property and that she found a packet of Sarah Ponsonby's notes to Sir William carefully put away in a pocket book.

It is probable that Mrs. Goddard's executors, when she died, found the Diary and Sarah's notes; as Sarah was living they would naturally send her own notes to her. As the rest of the Diary contained an account of events that had taken place at Woodstock as well as letters from Lady Betty, they would probably send these to Woodstock.

We know from the journal that Mrs. Tighe was alive in 1789; she would then be fifty-six and her daughter Caroline would be twenty-one. This appears to be a reasonable conjecture of how they came to possess the Goddard Diary.